Marching Schools Forward

Published in 2019 by Connor Court Publishing Pty Ltd
Copyright © Cheryl Lacey 2019

All rights reserved. No part of this book may be reproduced or transmitted in any form or by any means, electronic or mechanical, including photocopying, recording or by any information storage and retrieval system, without prior permission in writing from the publisher.

Connor Court Publishing Pty Ltd
PO Box 7257
Redland Bay QLD 4165

sales@connorcourt.com
www.connorcourtpublishing.com.au
Phone 0497 900 685

ISBN: 9781925826647

Front Cover Design: Maria Giordano
Front Cover Photo:
Printed in Australia

For Peter

Footprints of friendship and freedom,

dignity and trust.

God Bless

Marching Schools Forward

Discussions on the direction of Australian education

Cheryl Lacey

Connor Court Publishing

Table of Contents

	Foreword	9
	Introduction	13
	How to Use This Book	19
	20 Principles at a Glance	23

Section 1: The Fundamentals of Agreement

1	Principle 1: It Begins With the Language of Agreement	27
2	Principle 2: Australian Schools *not* Schools in Australia	33
3	Principle 3: The Matter of Law for Leaders and Learners	41
4	Principle 4: Education has Purpose Meaning and Impact	47
5	Principle 5: Diverse Ability – The Dignified Currency	53

Section 2: Free Australian Schools

6	Principle 6: There's Difference in Schools, Schooling and Education	61
7	Principle 7: Have an Educational Philosophy	67
8	Principle 8: Agree on a Stable Curriculum	73
9	Principle 9: Have Clear Boundaries with Flexible Frontiers	81
10	Principle 10: Honour Discipline and Freedom Follows	87

Section 3: Interdependent Relationships

11	Principle 11: Forget Partnerships - Nurture Genuine Relationships	95

12	Principle 12: Home - The First Priority	99
13	Principle 13: Lead Schools by Working Beside Families	105
14	Principle 14: Pedagogy - The Heartbeat of Every Classroom	113
15	Principle 15: Child and Student Are Not Synonymous	121

Section 4: Learning to Teach: Teaching to Learn

16	Principle 16: Diversify Teacher Quality	127
17	Principle 17: Negotiate on Merit	137
18	Principle 18: The Flexible Home-School-Work-Life Agreement	145
19	Principle 19: Assess and Report with More Than One Metric	151
20	Principle 20: Fund Suitability - Collect the Interest	161

A Final Note	171
Acknowledgements	173

Foreword

Are Australian schools marching forwards or backwards? It is old fashioned to use the word 'march', for most children no longer assemble in line and then march into their school rooms. But in a real sense they still march to the sound of a hidden drum. The drumbeat expresses a mix of modern ideologies and the latest rule-books.

At the federal election in 2019, education was said to be an important topic. But insofar as there was public debate about schools, it was mainly about money and rarely about the sound of the hidden drum.

Cheryl Lacey, a Melbourne consultant in education, ponders this vital question: how effective are schools? Her pithy book examines mainly the government or state schools which together form one of the biggest employers in the nation. Their payroll dwarfs that of Woolworths and Telstra. For most young Australians between the ages of five and eighteen, the waking hours are affected more by teachers than by any other people except their parents. For thousands of dysfunctional families, the teachers virtually serve as parents for five days of the week.

In the late nineteenth century our schools were successful by world standards. I have the strong impression that the teaching profession then, compared to today, attracted a larger share of the available talent amongst the school-leavers. At heavy expense the governments built thousands of schools and often a school-house for the teacher. The challenge of vast distances was largely met, except for Aboriginal children living in the far outback. Despite the high obstacles, we were one of the first lands to make education compulsory and free.

In contrast, Australian schools, as judged by the outside world, have become less competitive during the last dozen years. In literacy and numeracy, Australian students cannot match those in several East Asian countries. Knowledge of science has also suffered. And yet it was in 2007 that Kevin Rudd and Julia Gillard promised to launch what they called an education revolution that would '**create one of the most highly educated and skilled nations on Earth.**'

What happened to this revolution? Cheryl reveals that today's employers are often appalled at the illiteracy of numerous teenagers seeking work. After ten years of schooling, they cannot even fill in the application form. Such is the complaint of various managers of fast-food cafes and shops. Incidentally most teenagers who, passing the test, serve part-time in that industry, are usually impressive.

It is an eye-opener to learn that schooling, in practice, is no longer compulsory. Absenteeism and truancy are on the large scale. If you read carefully the major newspapers and watch the best television news, you probably gain the impression that the failure to attend school is a special problem for Aboriginal children in the outback. No, it is also a pressing problem in many suburbs and large country towns in mainstream Australia.

Of the larger workforces in Australia the teaching profession is untypical because it employs a majority of females: perhaps three of every four teachers are women. While it rejoices in the presence of thousands of dedicated and capable female and male teachers, it also employs many who are passengers. To dismiss an incompetent or dreary teacher is a long and difficult project. Dissatisfaction within the teaching profession is widespread. In Victorian government schools nearly half of the teachers, we are told, 'leave the job' within five years. Presumably many leave because they find a better-paid or more congenial job elsewhere but big numbers leave because they are discontented or frustrated.

Universities are also culprits. Many are known to tolerate low standards. Public-spirited academics privately are alarmed that they are compelled to give a pass mark to students who deserve to be failed. Some of these 'failures' re-invent themselves and pop up as classroom teachers.

This stimulating discussion-book is studded with suggestions and proposed remedies. One of the book's messages is that the teacher is all-important. The capable, enthusiastic teacher is amongst the nation's greatest assets. The third-rate teacher is a public liability but is rarely dismissed or sent into early retirement. At one time, 'inspectors' regularly visited schools, usually arriving without prior notice, and watched teachers at work and evaluated them and their students. Now, we are informed, a school's teaching team tends to assess itself.

At the other end of an Australian town or suburb, a local football or netball team often sets a higher standard than does the school. A successful sporting club dismisses or downgrades players who are not up to standard. Such a club also applauds and even enthrones the champion player. I am expressing in my own way what is one of the book's strongest messages.

Professor Geoffrey Blainey AC

Introduction

Ideas and concepts are the true power behind progress, innovation and civil society. They provide us with genuine platforms for robust debate, research and investment. This is of particular importance when it comes to education.

While many ideas have led to white papers, revolving door consultations, fads and ideologies, the truth is we still have a school system that compromises the lives of our children.

Previous reforms have included local and isolated change; others have come from worldwide movements affecting international school systems and millions of communities, including our own. Despite best intentions, every reform since compulsory education began in 1872 has eventually lost favour. The reason for this, however, may well be the key to lasting positive change. Reformists have failed to challenge the top-down political and bureaucratic use of compulsory schooling as a mechanism to control families.

This is the challenge offered in this book. Do we want stagnation or real reform? Bureaucracy and top-down control or unapologetic decentralisation? Nothing less than a complete overhaul of the State school system will clear away the decay that has been allowed to spread through the education portfolio, and every other government portfolio, particularly since the 1970s.

Some might say finding fault is easy, and they're right. That's the point. But if the system has failed one child, one family, one teacher or one school, it has the power to fail them all.

To develop potential solutions has been a challenge. Not everyone will agree with what's offered, and that's ok. The goal is not to have agreement. The ultimate purpose is to enable every child to have an authentic education– and that requires having better choices.

Just as challenging has been to find a way to simplify the complexity of education and present it in a format that is accessible to many different readers – parents, teachers, business owners, bureaucrats and policy makers.

Moving Forward to Fundamentals

Two questions must always be asked: Why must we change? How must we change? These questions keep the spotlight on this fundamental formula:

Diagram A: Sensible School Reform

Let's be clear: reform does not mean increased spending. Quite the contrary. *Sensible* reform involves:

1. Stability: Why undo, remove or replace what is working well?
2. Reduction: How might we reduce less-than-productive elements, including unnecessary spending?

3. Adjustment: How can we adjust existing strategies, before considering the need to increase resources?
4. Expansion: Why is this increase necessary?

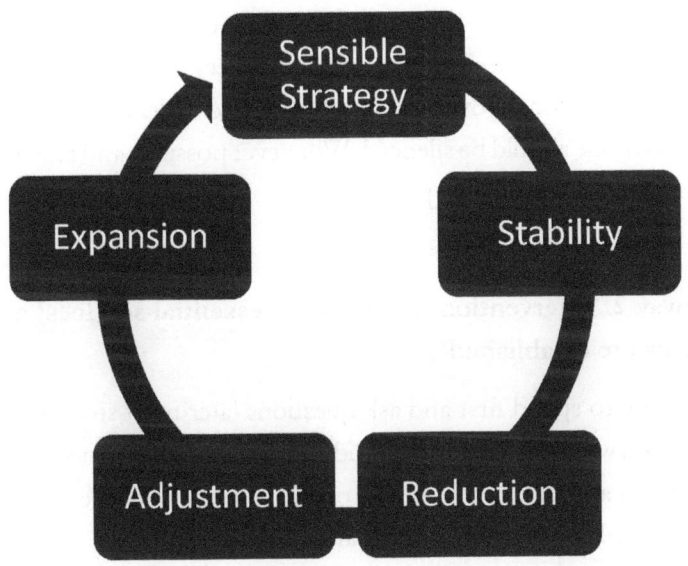

Diagram B: Core Strategy Considerations

Simultaneous Pathways to Reform

Enthusiasm for change, urgency created by political timetables, and the demands of unions and other industry voices, can force the enactment of premature *ad hoc* reform. The longevity of any reform of value, particularly system-wide reform, essentially requires parallel progress along **3 pathways**.

Pathway 1. Accord: encourage participation to prevent discontent

Everyone must be part of the action. That way, the consistent demand for 'more', every time reforms occur, will cease. Involvement creates trust, and a greater desire for ownership over that which every individual can contribute. Everyone deserves to belong, to be responsible and seek fulfilment. The voices of teachers, parents, workplaces, unions, government at State and federal level must be heard. No-one should be silenced. Whenever possible, and reasonable, we must have consultative processes.

Pathway 2. Intervention: cut back to 'essential services' as key reforms are established

The desire to spend first and ask questions later must stop. Shooting for reform without maintaining student progress in the process, results in children and families falling through the cracks unnecessarily. The fundamentals of sensible reform are found here.

Pathway 3. Innovation: take action

System wide reform can be executed only through cross portfolio involvement. The 20 principles found in this book are thought starters – the backbone to support system-wide reform.

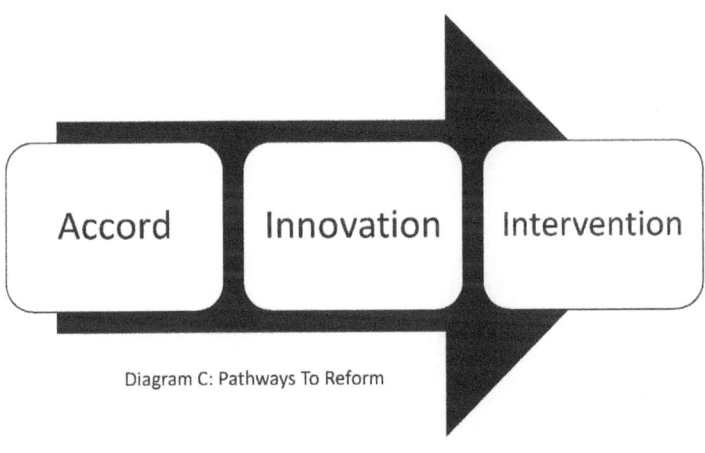

Diagram C: Pathways To Reform

Make no mistake, reform *will* have consequences. And our choices rarely have consequences whose effects are limited to ourselves. We must keep in mind, however, that for individuals to succeed, for families to thrive, and for society to be harmonious and to enjoy personal freedoms, we must accept personal responsibility. And that begins with a solid and meaningful education, supported by a proud and loyal government. We must remember, too, that to fail one child is to fail an entire family and its network of support.

Education in Victoria has gone backwards. But the trend can be reversed. To make that happen we need the will of the people and the politicians, and a genuine belief in what is possible. We cannot choreograph the future, but we can certainly be prepared for it.

How to Use This Book

We like to make things complicated. But we shouldn't. With regard to school education there are two possible strategies:

1. Make things so simple that when problems arise they can be easily resolved.
2. Make things so complex that when problems arise, they are hidden by more problems disguised as solutions.

Most of us experience the second option. And why? Because school education is personal. It's an emotional hot potato. It's much easier to avoid involvement when problems present themselves. That way, regardless of what action has been taken, we allow ourselves to believe the problem has been solved. Quite often, though, it hasn't. Solutions to a problem often lead to the creation of another problem. Imagine the alternative. What if the solutions to a problem could lead to new possibilities? That's optimistic thinking. And it's exactly the way to approach this book.

The 20 Principles at a Glance

At the beginning of the book, you will find a list of the **20 Principles**, each with a **Key Solution**.

Every principle intends to have an impact on devolution, shared responsibility and decision making – on families, schools, Federal and State governments and the local region.

Read these outlines and select the specific principles you might want to focus on; each principle has its own section in the text. Or read the book from beginning to end, and think about them all.

Looking More Closely

The book offers more detail on the 20 Key Principles, and aims to unravel some, but not all, of the complexities associated with school education. Each principle is described in words and diagrams and includes the following:

- An introductory quotation
- A story to set the scene
- An overview of the principle, which might include some historical background, anecdotes, statistics or a series of explanations.
- A key problem
- One or more consequences of the key problem
- A key solution
- Other possibilities

A Workbook Approach

Use the book as a workbook. The principles are in no particular order. Any one of them can be a starting point for re thinking and reassessing issues such as school suitability, or lack of choice. Copy the principles, take notes, write down questions or develop and improve those already listed. The ideas can be thought starters for further study, or for initiating local reform. They might serve as background for writing letters to local Members of Parliament.

Philosophers have pondered education for centuries. The work of two philosophers, in particular, has influenced the development of this book. The first, economic and moral philosopher Adam Smith (1723-1790), held the view that the wealth of a nation was not found in the hoarding of natural resources, but consisted of the productive activity of its people. The second, Mortimer Adler (1902–2001), an author and educational philosopher, believed that education was a lifelong process and should be a demonstration of choice. He also held the view that the purpose of being educated was to be a good citizen, to have freedom from control and freedom of circumstance. Had these philosophers met, there would have been much to discuss. Let's do so on their behalf.

20 Principles at a Glance

Each principle as listed identifies key problems and noteworthy solutions. Reading the 20 principles offers an overall insight into the broader implications of continued stagnation or the opportunity for critical reform. You play a major role in Australian education. After digesting these principles, problems and solutions you must choose to be an activist or pacifist. Which will it be? Marching Schools Forward isn't simply a book. It's a movement that begins with this overview.

Principle 1: It Begins With the Language of Agreement

Key Problem: Many have lost sight of the real value of English as Australia's shared language of agreement.

Key Solution: Agree on the meaning and intent behind ideas and concepts relating to education reform.

Principle 2: Australian Schools not Schools in Australia

Key Problem: The omission of education, in Australia's First Charter of Justice, has plagued the nation and put Judeo-Christian values at risk.

Key Solution: An independent body to develop a course on Western Civilisation and Ethics.

Principle 3: The Matter of Law for Leaders and Learners

Key Problem: The State is essentially equipped to fund its own defence in all matters related to State public schools. Any other party in any legal dispute must also fund itself.

Key Solution: New mandated course work on Schools and the Law for teachers and Principals to achieve certification.

Principle 4: Education has Purpose Meaning and Impact

Key Problem: Compulsory school attendance takes precedence over the provision of education.

Key Solution: Decentralise compulsory school education and invest in education services across portfolios.

Principle 5: Diverse Ability – The Dignified Currency

Key Problem: Compulsory school attendance is currently the only standard criterion for inclusion.

Key Solution: Replace the concept of disability with the concept of diverse ability opening funding and grants opportunities across portfolios.

Principle 6: There's Difference in Schools, Schooling and Education

Key Problem: Governments appear to limit the concepts of school and education to school related bricks and mortar determined by the government.

Key Solution: Schools to become centres of lifelong education open for 52 weeks of the year - After hours negotiated with community.

Principle 7: Have an Educational Philosophy

Key Problem: In schools there is often conflict between educational philosophy (theory) and the ability to apply it (practice).

Key Solution: All schools provide stable curriculum complemented by autonomous philosophy and specialisms at school level.

Principle 8: Agree on a Stable Curriculum

Key Problem: There is no stable stable curriculum that requires teachers and students to meet a particular standard.

Key Solution: National level of English language, mathematics, health and physical education, Western Civilization – Inspectorate monitored.

Principle 9: Have Clear Boundaries with Flexible Frontiers

Key Problem: The Bureaucracy has a monopoly on families with children of compulsory school age.

Key Solution: Tiered curriculum at National, State and Local Level.

Principle 10: Honour Discipline and Freedom Follows

Key Problem: Schools lack discipline and have the power to deny families their services.

Key Solution: Marry schools and their communities with a similar structure to State law enforcement agencies.

Principle 11: Forget Partnerships - Nurture Genuine Relationships

Key Problem: The only real partnership in education is between the State and the unions.

Key Solution: Schools can employ from State government pool or independent teachers not affiliated with the teacher's union.

Principle 12: Home - The First Priority

Key Problem: Competing loyalties compromise the intended purpose of libertarian free schooling.

Key Solution: Use database to 'Join Up' relevant services to meet client's needs.

Principle 13: Lead Schools by Working Beside Families

Key Problem: School education is compromised by a Principal's diverse responsibilities and priorities.

Key Solution: 3 Tiered Leadership model – Instructional Leader, Chief Executive Officer, Family Liaison Officer.

Principle 14: Pedagogy - The Heartbeat of Every Classroom

Key Problem: Teacher performance is not measured.

Key Solution: Teachers present pedagogy for quarterly review. Adjustments made in teaching, assessment and service providers.

Principle 15: Child and Student Are Not Synonymous

Key Problem: Family life is entering the public domain.

Key Solution: Family Liaison Officer key communicator with family on matters of the 'child'.

Principle 16: Diversify Teacher Quality

Key Problem: Universities have a monopoly on education degrees and certification.

Key Solution: Establish Teachers Colleges and Common Schools in every School Region.

Principle 17: Negotiate on Merit

Key Problem: Enterprise agreements place unions in control of teacher performance.

Key Solution: Establish a tiered wages system. Base income on a stable curriculum, supplemented by additional services.

Principle 18: The Flexible Home-School-Work-Life Agreement

Key Problem: The school year is inconsistent with flexible work practices.

Key Solution: Introduce staggered timetables from 8.00am to 6.00pm – offered 52 weeks of the year.

Principle 19: Assess and Report with More Than One Metric

Key Problem: Year 12 is the yardstick for workplace value and further study.

Key Solution: Certificates of achievement for stable curriculum, curriculum specialisms and community electives - not year level.

Principle 20: Fund Suitability - Collect the Interest

Key Problem: Funding is distributed to schools not to students.

Key Solution: Introduce national 'Educare' funding to provide rebates for families to access registered service providers across multiple portfolios.

Principle 1:

It Begins With the Language of Agreement

The purpose of all interactions is to understand and be understood.

Mai was born in Thailand. At 3 years and 10 months, she became my daughter. As well as making preparations for travel and the legalities of adoption, I purchased a number of practical resources I could use to build a rapport with her, and begin the process of teaching her the English language. An alphabet book, coloured plastic bracelets, linking blocks, balloons and crayons were part of the small collection.

Every day, from morning through to bedtime, I counted to 10, sang the same tunes, pointed to colours and repeated familiar words over and over. By day 7, Mai could count to 10 and name all 6 colours on her plastic bracelets.

When I brought her back in Australia, more toys were available and music filled the house. I engaged her in everyday experiences and shared activities, including cake making, tidying her bookshelf and doing the gardening. After just 6 weeks, she could sing the Alphabet Song and Jingle Bells. She also began to turn the pages of her favourite books and read them confidently, despite her limited vocabulary. Mai was well on the way to having a sense of belonging and personal fulfilment.

Vocabulary

We all have our own unique vocabulary. We acquire our vocabulary when we read and listen. We access it, and use it, whenever we speak and write. Just as importantly, when we produce words accurately, in conversations or in writing, we make sure others can create meaning from our intended messages.

Ideas and Concepts

Our vocabulary is rich with words that have evolved over time. Take for example the word 'chair'. It comes from the Greek word *kathedra*, via the latin cathedar, and the French chaire, which means the Bishop's seat or throne. Over time, with regular use, 'chair' became a term used to reference other seats beyond the church, while in English *kathedra* evolved into 'cathedral', the 'seat' of a bishop's power. Today, when we hear the word 'chair', we might not picture the original concept of a throne, but we certainly wouldn't picture a stool or a bench.

Language in Schools

Students bring to school a rich and wide repertoire of ideas and concepts. Some remain the same, while others evolve, particularly when combined with new ideas introduced through the standard curriculum. The concept of 'family' is a good example. For decades it was widely accepted that a family was a nuclear group consisting of mum, dad and their offspring. Today there are many recognised family structures. A fundamental understanding of any original idea is the first step towards acquiring and developing new concepts across all subject areas.

Compromising the English Language

In every subject area there is the need to read, write, speak, listen or record one's thinking. Less than 50% of Australian teachers, however, have a specialisation in English as a part of their training. Added to this, schools receive a financial loading to cater for students who speak a language other than English. The goal is to provide additional support for them to become competent users of English, but less than 10% of teachers are qualified to teach these students, and less than 10% of teachers have themselves studied a second language.

Understanding

Language underpins everything – our ideas, our concepts, our making of meaning and our communication. Our common language is English. The inherent value of a strong understanding of English is the ability and freedom it gives us to communicate in depth and with full understanding.

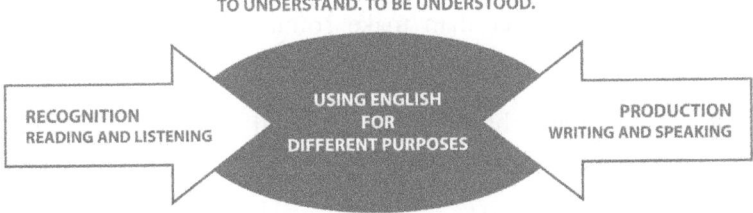

Diagram 1: Language and Understanding

If we don't have that understanding, the meaning of messages conveyed or received can be murky or misinterpreted. There's also the risk that ideas or concepts are not fully realised, or not sufficiently examined in terms of their merit or intent.

To feel a sense of belonging, to make a responsible contribution to society and to achieve self-fulfilment, competency in English – Australia's language of agreement – is vital for everyone.

The Problem

Many have lost sight of the real value of English as Australia's shared language of agreement.

The Consequences

- The Australian Curriculum does not include any definitive statements on *what* students should achieve, in English.
- Students progress from one school year to the next regardless of the standard of English they have attained.
- Schools rely on products, programs and popular learning methods rather than make sound and informed teaching decisions.
- Technology has all but erased handwriting, writing composition and rich oral discussion.
- Employers face increasing numbers of illiterate applicants.

Key Solution

Agree on the meaning and intent behind ideas and concepts relating to education reform.

Other Possible Solutions

- Develop 6 key stages of achievement in English.
- Revert to a graded (e.g. A-E) system of reporting in primary schools. (stage 1-3)
- Introduce certificates of attainment in English in secondary settings. (stage 4-6)
- Introduce a choice of strands of English – for example, non-fiction genre and English literature for Years 9 to 12. (stage 5 – 6))
- Introduce into schools a range of English language classes for the general public.
- Remove second languages from the standard Australian Curriculum and offer them as electives.

Principle 2:

Australian Schools not Schools in Australia

Our values and beliefs govern our behaviour.

Alison was raised as a Catholic. She had a Religious Instruction class every Tuesday morning at her local State school, and attended Sunday School until the end of Grade 4. She went to a State public secondary school and later obtained a Diploma of Education from a Teacher's College.

When Alison graduated, teaching positions for graduates were scarce. Her first step was to register for a position at a State school. She also applied to some independent schools, one of which was an Islamic school. Dressed respectfully in her regular Western attire, she arrived at the school. After a polite interview, she was advised that her dress code had come as a surprise. She didn't get the job.

Thirty years later, the Christian school that Alison's daughter attended altered its uniform selection to include a gender-neutral line. The impetus for doing this was a Muslim student who was working through identity problems regarding its sexuality.

Since the First Fleet sailed into Botany Bay in 1788, Australian schooling has been dogged by issues related to Judeo-Christian traditions. The penal colony had one rule of law – the First Charter of Justice. It articulated law and order, but no official provision was made for education; neither had schoolteachers arrived with the First Fleet.

The colony included 36 children: 19 were the offspring of the marines and 17 were from convict parents. These children of the privileged and the poor lived together and played together. By 1800 there were almost 1000 children living in the rapidly growing colonies. The need for schools, to provide education and to stem vagrancy, became clear.

Our First Instructors

Well-educated convicts were initially entrusted to fill the urgent need for instructors. Churches of many denominations ensured a sense of community and, religion played an important role in moral instruction. Most children attended Sunday school and church each week. Denominational and church schools were established and other trial school systems were also implemented.

The Ten Commandments

Every society lives by a set of morals or core values. They guide our behaviour and serve as the fundamental measure for interpreting human interaction and its impact. As a Western civilisation, Australia derives its particular system of values and principles from the Ten Commandments.

- You shall have no other gods before Me.
- You shall make no idols.
- You shall not take the name of the Lord your God in vain.
- Keep the Sabbath day holy.
- Honour your father and your mother.

- You shall not murder.
- You shall not commit adultery.
- You shall not steal.
- You shall not bear false witness against your neighbour.
- You shall not covet.

The slow cumulative work of innumerable citizens from all walks of life contributed to the formation of the nation and of each State and Territory. That the separation of powers was achieved without bloodshed is evidence that, despite our differences, we are deeply rooted in our Judeo-Christian beliefs.

State Public Schools and Secular Education

Victoria inherited the National Education system from New South Wales. Land distribution, diversity in population, and financial support for some denominations over others were of great concern. Financial and religious positions determined access to education. Political and religious battles began. The loss of trust resulted in a major fallout between government, parents, and faith groups. A centralised public system was born, and the Public Education Act was passed. It was the beginning of government control over schools, the purpose of which was to provide free, compulsory and secular education.

Local control of schools, once shared by families and the community, was removed and financial aid to church-based schools was abolished.

Secular education was intended to provide fundamental teachings in English and Mathematics, without the influence of any one overriding Christian influence.

Declining Values

The use of faith as political weaponry has permeated our schools and has all but replaced the genuine meaning of secular education. Instead, a new cult of anti-religious, self-serving minorities are chipping away at our established values. Schools can take the blame for the declining respect for Judeo-Christian values, and their impact on the teaching of history and its ramifications.

Our future relies very much on our past. It depends on the passing on of accurate accounts of events, sacrifices and changes that have so far ensured our Western way of life. Our society needs this measuring stick by which our behaviours can be viewed, judged, supported and encouraged. Australian schools play a critical role in honouring the accuracy and value of these standards.

The Place of Islam

Our first public school buildings were places of instruction and worship. Separation of church and state encouraged people of all faiths to study and to worship. There was no intention to influence thought that would undermine our broader Judeo-Christian values. There is no place for such thought in Australian schools today. Islam is a doctrine that does not separate church from state. Islamic schools, like any other denominational schools, have the right to observe and teach their faith. In 2007, a two-day conference, was held in South Australia. Its purpose was to develop a standardised national Islamic-Saudi curriculum that would be a world first in the Western world. Islamic educators claim students want to explore 'real life issues' at greater depth, to learn 'how to live in society', as 'functional Muslims', and to gain the knowledge and skills to 'apply what is being learned.' They say these desires support the objectives of the Australian Curriculum Assessment and Reporting Authority (ACARA). Muslims would then have a solid education on the four 'madhhabs', or major schools of Islamic thought, which are currently limited to personal practice, due to Australian law.

We must better understand Islam and its similarities to our beliefs and values; we must also understand where the differences lie. To remain ignorant of Islam is to accept the possibility of chaos and destructive behaviour between individuals and groups, when differences are neither understood nor respected.

Unique cultural identities, values and practices in our country are threads in a wider, clearly defined Australian cultural tapestry. All schools have a responsibility to convey the feeling of pride in, and the sense of belonging to, a nation that offers so much to so many. Judeo-Christian values are central to this sense of belonging.

To register, and fund, any school that does not respect Judeo-Christian values is to fund the undermining of those values and the fundamental principles on which Western civilisation is built.

Diagram 2: Judeo Christian Principles For Registration

Western Civilisation and Ethics

We have our own distinctive traditions and culture, including the English language, and laws that are consistent with the values of Australian society. We subscribe to inviting immigrants to belong – freely and genuinely – to Australia. And we expect *all* of its citizens to value its culture, become articulate in its language, and respect its laws.

As human beings we are both body and spirit. Our behaviours and beliefs are challenged in every decision we make, every day. To value our language, identify with our culture and respect our laws is to know what it is to value the ethics woven into our daily lives. No-one is perfect, or wholly imperfect. Everyone, however, is a reflection of another. Our ethical footprint is followed, trampled on and recreated daily.

A society's attitude towards children is a gauge of its broader social and moral concerns. Schools should not be measured by the money spent, the results achieved, or the competition encouraged. School is an equaliser, where personal lives can be forgotten, even if for just a short while, so that children can embrace the English language and their place in our nation, and begin to evolve – developing self, and contributing to others.

Ethical behaviour in schools begins with respect for individuality and compassion for others. These are central to the Judeo-Christian beliefs and traditions on which Australia and Australian schools were founded.

The Problem

The omission of education, in Australia's First Charter of Justice, has plagued the nation and put Judeo-Christian values at risk.

The Consequences

- Australian schools are controlled by six different State Constitutions.
- Parents are faced with moral and ethical inconsistencies across schools and school systems.
- Values-based education is a matter of personal and school choice.
- Teachers must manage conflicting religious, moral and ethical viewpoints.
- Schools compete for enrolment using selective moral and ethical characteristics as tag lines and advertising campaigns.
- Chaplaincy programs are funded by the Commonwealth, and administered by the State; there are opt-in or opt-out clause for individual schools.

Key Solution

An independent body to develop a course on Western Civilisation and Ethics.

Other Possible Solutions

Western Civilisation and Ethics:

- Included in the stable Australian Curriculum
- As a compulsory unit of pre-service training
- As a specialist degree, for those who wish to qualify as chaplains and educators in history and ethics.
- Included in the curriculum as a pre-requisite for Commonwealth funding and State registration.

Languages other than English become electives, and are not funded by the Commonwealth.

Principle 3:

The Matter of Law for Leaders and Learners

Does duty of care mean protecting the children of others or protecting ourselves and our own children?

Nicola was a Year 2 teacher, working in a suburban State primary school. Her husband, Matt, was a dentist. Their two children attended the local State primary school. A serious case of misconduct took place at the children's school. The breach had implications for the entire community. Nicola and Matt joined a group of parents who campaigned to resolve the matter. After attending several meetings, Nicola and Matt suddenly became quiet. Nicola informed another parent that she couldn't campaign with parents at one school and be an employee at another. She feared for her job and chose to stop campaigning.

Schools and the Law

Schools operate within a complex web of Federal and State laws that have an impact on the rights and responsibilities of school leaders, students, teachers, parents and others connected to school-based education.

Many of the issues schools must address – professional conduct, student injury, child custody matters, freedom of expression, mandatory reporting and enterprise bargaining –

require an understanding of the law. Then there are the common recommendations and advice for school staff, such as 'Don't touch children', or 'Don't be left alone with a child'. From where does this come? Is it overkill? What might be the consequences of ignoring this advice?

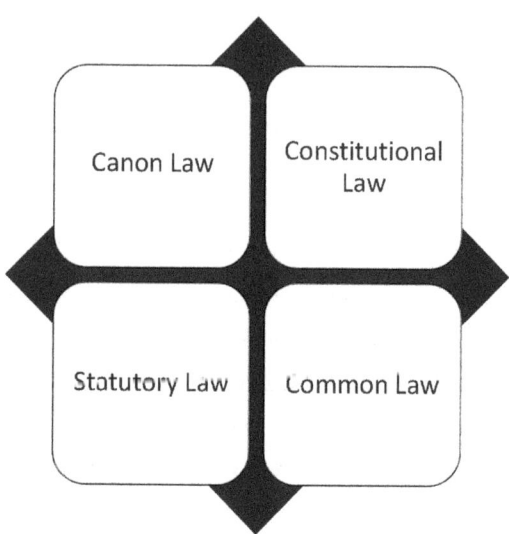

Diagram 3: Four Types Of Law

Canon Law

Canon Law is the body of law that regulates the major Christian Churches. It is determined by ecclesiastic authorities, and is not static, reflecting social, political, economic and cultural changes. It has influenced the development of Western civil and common law – e.g. the principle of 'innocent until proven guilty' can be attributed to a long held interpretation of Canon Law.

Constitutional Law

Constitutional Law is Australia's supreme law. Its primary source is the Australian Constitution, which established the Federal system of government that distributes powers between the Commonwealth government and the six autonomous States.

Common Law

Common Law is the law developed over time. When hearing cases, judges apply what they believe to be sound principles of law. Common law develops as a result of judges' decisions, based on these principles.

Statutory Law

Statutory law is created by government, through elected legislators and the official legislative process. Courts are responsible for interpreting and enforcing statutory law, but they cannot create it.

Victorian Law

Victoria's first Education Act, *The Education Act 1872*, outlined among other things, the purpose of free, compulsory and secular education, the role of teachers and their remuneration and the standard curriculum. It also included the use of school buildings, scholarships beyond the standard curriculum and the language of agreement for the *Certificate for a child being sufficiently educated*. It is 6 pages long, and a fascinating read.

Today, Victoria's Education Training and Reform Act, 2006 (version 75) is 791 pages long. If that's not enough, there are a further 129 pages of the Australian Education Act, 2013 – even though the Federal government does not employ any teachers, and does not register or operate any schools. Many other Acts add to the complexity of schools and the law; all of them affect families and school employees.

In less than 150 years, Victorian Education has shifted from a doctrine of optimism to a legal quagmire. Its original purpose and its commitment to a free education for every child have been strangled by an obsession for more legislation. Respect for our moral footprint has all but vanished.

Relationships and the Law

Thomas and Daniel were high school students. Their parents had separated, and had shared responsibility for the boys, putting in place a 'week-about' strategy for their care and residential arrangements. The boys' mother worked full-time. Their father arranged his schedule so that he worked 60-80 hours during the weeks when the boys were with their mother, and worked only in school hours during the weeks they lived with him. He was well known in the community as the 'school dad' and an honorary member of the school mums' social club.

Then the mother's private circumstances changed. The father learned of the situation and, without warning, the boys' weekly arrangements with their father ceased, and they resided full time with their mother. There were no court papers relating to custody arrangements.

Not knowing what to do, the father went to the State high school his sons attended. He believed it would be a safe, neutral ground, where he could see them and to try to resolve the matter. When he arrived at the school, the father was told the school had a duty of care to protect the emotional wellbeing of their students. The principal denied the father access to his sons and the grounds for this action were not explained. The mother moved interstate with her sons. The father remains estranged from his children.

Schools are about relationships – between children, the parents responsible for raising them, and the employees charged with assisting in their education. Boundaries can be blurred and responsibilities can be compromised when duty of care is taken too literally or not taken seriously enough. The constant challenge is to determine whether, and when, one should and should not take action.

School systems have a bottomless pit of money and legal advice; families do not. It is, therefore, nearly impossible to know the extent of problems faced by schools and their clients.

On the other hand, knowledge of the relationship between schools and the law can bring preventative measures: measures that could outweigh expensive, distracting, time-consuming and destructive disputes.

The Problem

The State is essentially equipped to fund its own defence in all matters related to State public schools. Any other party in any legal dispute must also fund itself.

The Consequences

- Defending oneself against government is almost impossible
- The number of breaches of appropriate teacher conduct is unknown
- Families have no voice
- The school system has the power and money to destroy lives.

Key Solution

New mandated course work on *Schools and the Law* for teachers and principals to achieve certification.

Other Possible Solutions

- Create a unit of study on *School and the Law* as a compulsory component of pre-service teacher courses.
- Develop a course in *Educational Mediation*, to enable independent practitioners to specialise.
- Require principals to complete a major in a course on *School and the Law*. This would be included in a course for principal certification.
- Fund a partisan body charged with representing parents and other parties.

Principle 4:

Education has Purpose, Meaning and Impact

Reality is the measure that matters.

The owner of a local McDonald's franchise approached the local newspaper. His increasing frustration with low literacy capabilities of school age teenagers had finally prompted him to speak up. A regular stream of teens visits his store to apply for part-time positions. Many are unable to complete the application form. Some have learning disabilities, and are encouraged and supported to gain employment. He remains overwhelmed, however, by the many others who are nearing the end of compulsory schooling, but lack the fundamental skills to follow simple instructions or write legibly.

What is the purpose of education?

For centuries philosophers have sought answers to this question, and have also asked what it means to have a good education and how education relates to life and life's purposes. Some believe education should prepare us to enter the workforce. Others believe the purpose of education should be focused more on social, academic, cultural and intellectual development. We could then think critically, and debate with authority on issues of importance.

In reality, there is no right or wrong answer. Put simply, the purpose of education is to change people through teaching. The change involves *learning* or moving from not knowing to knowing. And, because learning is such a personal process, education has a different value and purpose for each of us. Most of us understand that learning happens continuously, over the course of a lifetime, as each individual thinks and feels and acts. The phrase *lifelong learning* signifies this understanding.

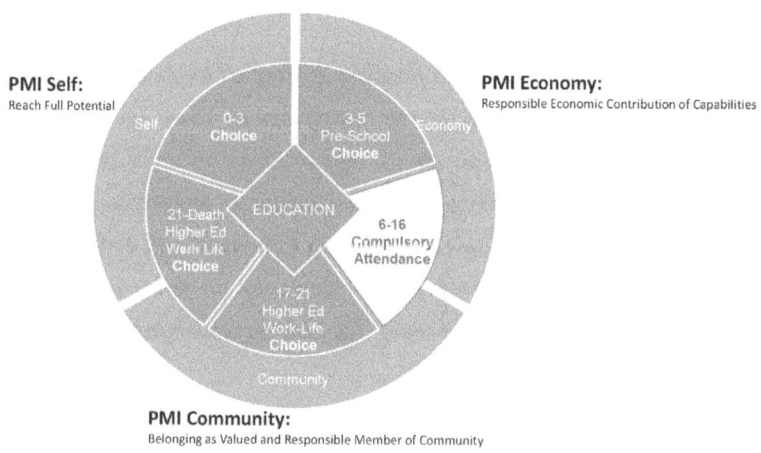

Diagram 4: Education From Birth To Death

Compulsory School Education

Free, compulsory and secular school education in Victoria began in 1872 from the doctrine of optimism. As a young, growing and dynamic nation, a view was put forward that every child should reach an agreed standard of competency in reading, writing and arithmetic.

Income, religion and social status should never be reasons for the denial of a child's right to achieve this agreed standard.

Free, compulsory and secular school education would be provided for every child aged 6-15 years. Not more than four hours per day, over 120 days per calendar year, would be allocated for this instruction. If children demonstrated the aptitude and enthusiasm for further learning, parents could pay teachers – as they would a tutor – for further study. A standard education, combined with the opportunity for further study would benefit the child, the family and the growing colony. It was the best of all possible worlds.

Today, in Victoria, attendance is compulsory for students aged from 6-17 years. The school day has expanded to 5 hours of instruction, the curriculum is overloaded, and the school year has lengthened to approximately 190 days. Teachers are no longer chosen, nor paid, by parents.

Compulsory school education is to enable students to:

- Find personal fulfilment
- Contribute to the economic security of self and nation
- Belong to, and be a valued as a responsible member of, the community

As these three aims indicate, compulsory school education is intended to teach students to be concerned with the affairs of the community in conjunction with the pursuit of their personal fulfillment and the meeting of personal responsibilities.

Every year, as VCE or Year 12 results are released, there is great celebration of the top performing students. Schools proudly showcase their results and use them as a promotional tool for securing future students. Billboards are displayed to highlight the school's best performers. Newspapers print lists of schools in chronological order from best to less so, judged by Year 12 student outcomes.

For students who have worked hard, improved their performance, but have not reached the top 5%, there is no public fanfare. And, for those who have reached the age of 17 and have little or no interest in the subjects on offer, the incentive to stay in school can vanish.

It must be remembered, that during the compulsory school years, there are many other influencers in students' lives; these influencers also have an impact on the intended aims of school education.

The Impact of School Education

When adults secure employment, they apply their fundamental capabilities to industry-specific requirements, to fulfil their work responsibilities. Over time, to maintain or improve their position, they will be expected to change and adapt to developments in their industry, and develop further capabilities. This requires continuous learning.

Teachers involved in compulsory school education can contribute to students' fundamental capabilities. They cannot provide future employees with industry-specific capabilities; neither can they foresee the changes decades in advance.

It would be naïve for any educational leader, politician or policy maker to suggest that all three aims were achievable for *every* individual student in our current centralised system.

What is possible, however, is agreement on the fundamental capabilities that must be achieved during the compulsory school years, in association with other influencers and interests. In other words, it's possible to develop a model that combines compulsory schooling with aptitude and interests of choice. This would pave the way for students to work hard, give back to the community, and strive for personal fulfilment.

The Problem

Compulsory school attendance takes precedence over the provision of education.

The Consequences

- The three aims are bundled into the same broad curriculum for teachers, students and schools.
- Compulsory school education is confused with compulsory school attendance.
- Spending on education, during the compulsory school years, is restricted to compulsory school education.
- Centralised bureaucracy has a monopoly on teaching individuals of compulsory school age.

Key Solution

Decentralise compulsory school education and invest in education services across portfolios.

Other Possible Solutions

- Invest in a range of teacher service providers – including services of choice, small business, tutors and elder mentors.
- Education services in standard curriculum funded for all ages.

Principle 5:

Diverse Ability – the Dignified Currency

With dignity there is light, no matter how dim.

A young man, in his early 20s, with a keen interest in sport, informed me he was disabled, and had three carers under the NDIS. Although he has been diagnosed as mildly autistic, and intellectually challenged, his manners and conduct in public are far beyond most young men of his age. He has a positive outlook and is conversational, particularly if you tap into matters of sport.

I have yet to meet anyone who has his range of knowledge and passion for sport. He knows all about cricket, football codes and basketball in Australia, NZ and the USA. He travels widely on public transport, and uses his Uber account, to participate as player and spectator. He's also in full-time employment. He is an extraordinary young man.

During a casual conversation, I suggested he wasn't disabled. His response was, 'Oh, yes I am. Mum says so'.

'I can't play basketball. I can't play football. I can't play cricket. But you can', I said.

He agreed.

'I don't know the rules of these sports. I couldn't tell you players' names or history, or talk about the coaches. I don't have any of the information you do', I said.

He agreed.

'I can, however, cook a 4-course meal, and I can write articles,' I added'.

He agreed.

'Well, in that case, we could say we're both disabled. But how about we agree, instead, that we have diverse ability'.

Diverse Ability

Everyone has the ability or the means to do something. Over the course of a lifetime we acquire additional abilities, and our existing abilities might change. Many develop and improve, some remain the same, and others decline or become less effective. We all have diverse ability.

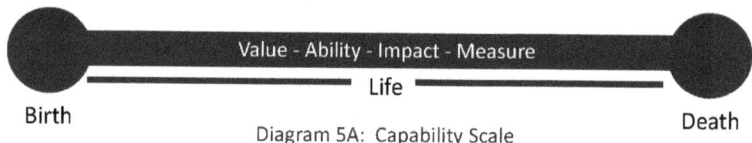

Diagram 5A: Capability Scale

Making Adjustments for Diverse Ability

In schools, teachers regularly attempt to adapt or adjust the standard curriculum and/or their practice to accommodate their own, and their students', different abilities. This might involve varying teaching methods, or creating different assessments to support different learning capabilities. A standard example would be to place students in different instructional groups for the teaching of reading strategies. Another common adjustment would be to allow students who are not comfortable with public speaking to make oral presentations to a small group of their peers, rather than to the whole class.

Over a 13-year period of compulsory school attendance, every student will experience some type of adjustment, just as teachers will need to make adjustments each year in all the subject areas in which they teach. Making adjustments is a natural part of the learning and teaching process.

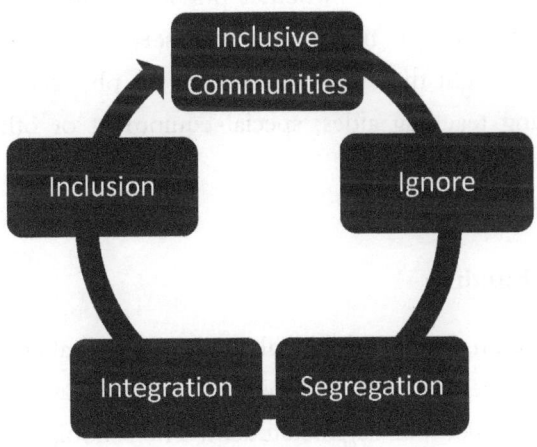

Diagram 5B: Delivering Inclusive Education For All

Disability in Schools

For decades, children living with disability were either ignored or segregated; they certainly couldn't attend mainstream schools. During the 1980s, the Victorian Department of Education introduced what was referred to as an Integration Program. This gave children with a disability the right to be enrolled in a mainstream school. The Integration Program has since been replaced with one of inclusion. In mainstream schools, enrolments of students with a disability have increased and the number of special schools has dramatically decreased.

It is not possible for all students to have the same experience of school. Inclusion, however, imposes on schools a legal obligation to ensure all students have the same opportunities and choices in their education.

In cases of disability – whether physical or intellectual – more complex adjustments might be necessary for some children. Adjustments might then involve adapting the physical environment, or employing teaching aides, special equipment or other essential resources.

Disability Funding

In some circumstances, additional funding for disability might also be available. The costs involved might range from just over $7,300 to more than $56,000 per eligible student. The school, in consultation with the parents, forms a student support group, which must determine the specific nature of the support required. Schools might be eligible for additional funding when they have enrolled students who present the following disabilities:

- Physical disability
- Visual impairment
- Severe behavioural disorders

- Intellectual disability
- Autism spectrum disorder
- Severe language disorders

It should be made clear, however, that not all students – including those presenting with these disabilities – are eligible for the same amount of funding. In some instances, no additional funding is available.

Impact of the Right to Attend

The National Disability Standards for Education have been developed to ensure all children of compulsory school age (6-17 years), including those living with a disability, have the same educational opportunities and choices, including the right to attend a mainstream school.

Maintaining a focus on disability, however, might mean other students are denied the adjustments necessary to cater for their diverse abilities. It affects, for example, students with a gift or talent, or students who are at a much lower than expected reading level, but who do not present with a disability. Situations like these do not attract additional funding and teachers do not always have the capabilities to manage diverse abilities.

As well as this, school settings outside the State school system – for example, a school for those with sight impairment, which is not listed, above, as a disability – are seen to be in breach of the students' Human Rights.

Mere school attendance does not guarantee the adjustment of a standard curriculum for every possible variation of disability or ability. While students are young, inclusion might seem the right strategy to employ; preparation for long-term needs such as employment and self-care, however, isn't part of any standard curriculum.

The problem

Compulsory school attendance is currently the only standard criterion for inclusion.

The consequences

- The value of special schools for attendance and specialised teaching has been compromised.
- Teachers in mainstream schools with general capabilities are expected to teach beyond their capabilities.
- For those managing a disability, there is a high rate of family breakdown.
- Many families must self-fund any required schooling that is outside current funding models.

Key Solution

Replace the concept of disability with the concept of diverse ability opening funding and grants opportunities across portfolios.

Other Possible Solutions

- Change the language so as to express positives. Remove *disability* and replace it with *diverse ability*

- Redistribute funding from the Department of Education and incorporate it into other portfolios, including the Department of Health, via targeted student support

- Expand opportunities for students with diverse abilities, including those who are gifted and talented

- Redistribute grants, including those to the not-for-profit sector, to fund specialised units for diverse abilities within State schools, and portable services, including specially equipped buses – particularly useful for regional schools (e.g. Life Education vans)

- Create a suite of courses and degrees in *Diverse Ability* for pre-service and in–service education.

Principle 6:

The Difference Between Schools, Schooling and Education

School, schooling and education. Three concepts that affect you for life.

Overlooking Albert Street, on five acres of land in East Melbourne, is St Patricks Cathedral. It is one of only two large-scale church constructions to be completed during the 19th century. It is built of bluestone from Footscray, its bells were imported from Europe, and its stained glass windows have been lovingly restored. Insurance premiums for the cathedral are estimated at $400 million per annum.

Its use is not limited to weekday and Sunday Masses. It is a meeting place, and open all hours of the day for private worship and prayer. It offers a scholarship program for choir members, and is a venue for weddings, funerals and baptisms. And let's not forget its importance for tourism: hundreds of visitors, most from overseas, come to the Cathedral every day.

Over the years, local churches might have lost some patrons but, like the Cathedral, their value, in terms of supporting faith and education, and providing a safe place of assembly, must never be forgotten.

Humble Beginnings

Like churches, our public schools are also valuable assets. Most occupy prime real estate in central locations right across the country.

Melbourne's first school – an Aboriginal school established in 1836 – was situated near the Botanical Gardens. Thomas Smith, the school's teacher, would later become the Lord Mayor of Melbourne.

About the same time, in 1837, Melbourne's first public building was constructed on the corner of William and Little Collins Streets. The cost was met by donations from citizens of various denominations. It was to be used for services on Sabbath and Sundays and as a school during the week. A ship's bell summoned the children to school and citizens to worship.

During Victoria's gold rushes just over a decade later, tents were used as schools and places of general worship.

Mass Schooling

Libertarians firmly believed that every child should have a basic education. It was clearly not possible for every community to raise sufficient funds to establish a school for every denomination; therefore the construction of 'free schools' began. As populations increased and money became scarce – particularly during times of war and depression – rented shops and church halls were used for the purpose. As new schools were built, old ones were converted for other purposes, including Mechanics Halls.

Investment

The provision of funds for education, from State and Federal governments, raises constant debate. The 'Building the Education Revolution' of 2010, where more than $16 billion was spent on design and construction of school refurbishments and halls, is one example. It was lauded as a great success and a means of combating unemployment in volatile times. In real terms, however, it guaranteed income for construction giants and employment in a limited number of industries. The design of new school wings also influenced school philosophy, teacher performance and, ultimately, student outcomes. The impact is still felt.

Whenever there is word of investment in education, it's generally understood to mean an investment in students and their education. This isn't necessarily the case. It can be, quite literally, an investment in bricks and mortar – school buildings and facilities.

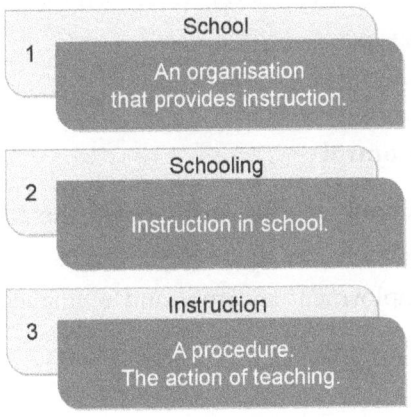

Diagram 6: Instruction Takes Place In Schools

Loss of Value

In February 2019, there were 2,256 schools in Victoria, of which 1,539 were Victorian State schools, with enrolments of just under 619,000 students and an average student teacher ratio of 22:1.

The Victorian State school system operates on a 40-week academic year. Generally speaking, there are 4 terms of 10 weeks each. In other words, schools are open for instruction for 40 weeks of the calendar year.

That means there are just over 28,000 empty classrooms for 12 weeks of the year, as well as unused libraries, halls, basketball courts, sports equipment and art rooms.

Flexible Facilities

Students enjoy camps, excursions, and incursions, where experts provide experiences that would not otherwise occur in schools. Flexible facilities add tremendous value. Schools can, and should, be flexible facilities too.

The Value of Control

The value of schools reaches well beyond the education portfolio. Investment in schools acts as a control mechanism, a law and order initiative, an employment measure and a financial investment for governments.

Problem

Governments appear to limit the concepts of school and education to school related 'bricks and mortar.'

The Consequence

- The major beneficiaries of investment in schools are those working in schools and the building and construction industries that work on them.

- The State government is the recipient of investment in schools.

Key Solution

Schools to become centres of lifelong education open for 52 weeks of the year - After hours negotiated with community.

Other Possible Solutions

- Register other facilities as schools – for example, camps, education vans
- Invest widely in sub-contracted education service providers to supplement school-based education.

Principle 7:

Have an Educational Philosophy

If you lean on someone who is leaning on someone else, you'll fall over.

At 3 years old, Ting began her transition from a physically active climbing enthusiast, to a disciplined and highly skilled elite gymnast. At age 5, she was invited to join an international squad. By Year 4, her training commitments had increased to 26 hours per week, and by Year 7, Ting's first year of secondary school, she was training for 30 hours each week. Her entire compulsory school education had, to that point, been part-time.

When she was 11, Ting's training time of 30 hours per week was almost one third more than a teacher's classroom teaching load. Her travelling time in the car was almost 8 times more than a teacher's lunch break. Despite that, her workload remained consistent with that expected of a student attending school full-time.

By the end of year 7, she was aware of gaps in her learning. Trying to keep up with school commitments and gymnastics meant she was burnt out. After 8 years of involvement, she quit gymnastics. Any desire to follow her dream had been suffocated by the demands of the crowded school curriculum.

A clear educational philosophy is generally defined as the body of knowledge and opinion on education that shapes the vision and mission of a school system, a school and its teachers.

Philosophies of the past continue to influence the range and nature of instructional methods that teachers use today. In some instances, particular approaches are considered more acceptable or necessary than others, and some are in conflict with others. Nevertheless, every philosophy, regardless of its value, is struggling to gain ground in an ever-growing bureaucracy. Ultimately, educational philosophy can be narrowed down to one core principle: learning and teaching, whether with a teacher-directed approach or a child-centred approach.

Monitorial Teacher-Directed Philosophy

The teacher-directed approach is best described by two methods of teaching developed in the 19th century: the Monitorial system and the Bell system. Influenced by the industrial revolution, these philosophies imitated methods employed in factories and in mass production. The architecture was simple: one large classroom was all that was required. One supervising teacher was in charge. Students sat at desks arranged in rows, and were placed according to their educational level, so that common exercises were easier to teach. Monitors, seated at the front of each row, would take instructions from the teacher and then hand out materials, work with students, and collect their work.

This teacher-directed model also featured rigid timetables that divided the day into lesson and non-lesson time by the ringing of a bell.

In many respects, the legacy of these industrial models remains in schools today. Timetables, bells, monitors, groupings according to ability and age, and vacations *en masse* are some obvious examples.

The most enduring legacy, however, is the economic use of human resources: one teacher is responsible for many students. And, given unions represent school employees *en masse*, you could say the industrial philosophy is alive and well in Victorian schools.

Child-Centred Philosophy

The child-centred model, on the other hand, is considered the oldest pedagogical philosophy, and is in total contrast with the industrial or teacher-centred model. The characteristics of this philosophy are that students of different ages and abilities are housed in the same space, but are engaged in individual and often different tasks at the same time. As they master each task, the teacher reviews the work and, if the evidence of learning is there, a new task is selected. This teaching model embodies a more personalised approach, and does not rely on formal arrangements, a standard curriculum or the application of formal assessments.

Common Sense

Variations of the teacher-centred and child-centred models have evolved into many different philosophies. Schools and individual teachers are encouraged to develop their own philosophies of education. Considering how bureaucracies control schools, however, this can lead to contradictions.

It must be made clear that, from an organisational point of view, Victorian schools are structured predominantly on features of the Monitorial and Bell systems. These school mandates, however, cannot adequately match the needs and capabilities of all students, particularly those with talents that lie outside the boundaries of the standard curriculum. And, while a child-centred approach implies having regard for the 'best interests of the child', this cannot be achieved given the way in which schools are currently organised.

The purpose of school is to contribute to the life of a child by assisting parents in the child's education. A school system, therefore, should place the parent and child at the centre of its philosophy and identify clearly what it can and cannot offer.

Identifying a Philosophy

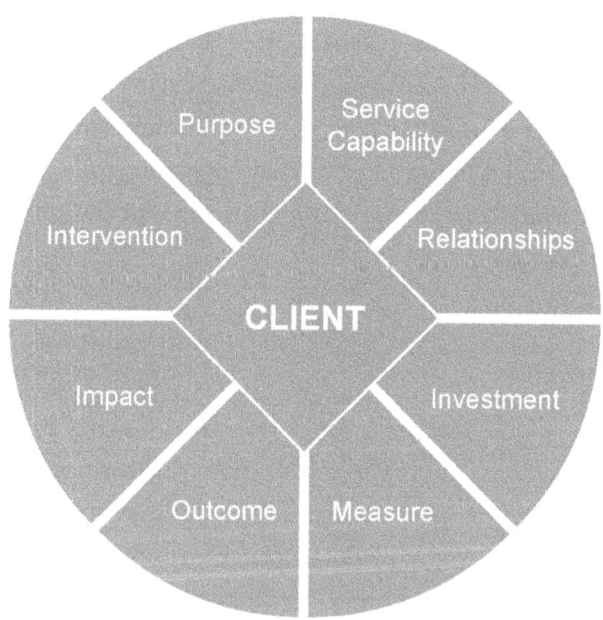

Diagram 7: Why And How We Serve

School systems need to address these questions:

1. What is the school's role in the life of the family?
2. What services can staff and facilities provide to families?

3. How can the family unit be better supported in its relationships with the school and other service providers?

4. For families, what are the relative advantages of investing in one school, rather than in a range of services provided elsewhere?

5. Which elements of the 'best interests of the child' can be measured by the system?

6. What is the expected outcome for a family after 13 years of compulsory schooling?

7. How are other portfolios affected by the performance of the school system?

8. At what point does the family have the right to intervene if the services provided by the system are not in the 'best interests of the child'?

A philosophy of education must be one that aims to provide value to the client (the family) by demonstrating the value of the educational services a school provides.

Problem

In schools there is often conflict between educational philosophy (theory) and the ability to apply it (practice).

Consequences

- Changes in leadership, at federal, state and school level, have an impact on educational philosophy.

- Competing ideologies have negative effects on the philosophy of compulsory school education.
- Schools and teaching staff do not necessarily share the same philosophy.
- Parents have no influence on philosophy in a centralised system.
- The 'best interests of the child' cannot be ensured when the standard curriculum and other offerings are tied to a bureaucratic system.

Key Solution

All schools provide stable curriculum complemented by autonomous philosophy and specialisms at school level.

Other Possible Solutions

- Certificate in *Educational Philosophy* compulsory component of pre-service teacher training.
- Certificate in *Leading Educational Philosophy* for principal certification
- Course developed for School Council members on educational philosophy
- Establishment of independent body to approve autonomous philosophy and offerings of individual schools.
- Establishment of independent body to approve autonomous philosophy of teachers.

Principle 8:

Agree on a Stable Curriculum

When you've learned the lyrics there's so much joy in singing along.

The Latin word curriculum means a 'course that is run'. However, our understanding of curriculum, which means 'that which is learned', goes back to the beginning of time, when hunters and gatherers taught other family members to hunt, fish, gather food, find water, carve rocks, and live with others. Learning was essentially about life and survival. We could almost say that hunters and gatherers established the first known curriculum – a curriculum for living. Schools, on the other hand, began as organisational structures. They provided a means of educating children en masse.

Free Instruction

In 1872, free instruction was introduced in Victoria for all children aged 6-15 years. It consisted of a standard curriculum: reading; writing; arithmetic; grammar; drill; and, where practicable, gymnastics. For girls there was the additional benefit of instruction in sewing and needlework. When they reached a particular *standard of education* in reading, writing and arithmetic, children would receive a certificate.

Teachers were paid their salary and remuneration based on students' results. Specialised instruction outside the standard curriculum was also available. Parents would be responsible for paying teachers these fees, a portion of which would go into consolidated funds to cover salaries for teaching the standard curriculum.

Extending the Standard

Instruction outside the standard curriculum expanded with the introduction of grammar schools, for students who demonstrated the capability and enthusiasm for study at University. High schools and technical schools were also established.

In 1942, as a wartime measure, there were fundamental changes made to Australia's tax system, which led to a reduction in the States' tax revenue. To provide education, States were forced to rely on a distribution of funds from the federal government. During the Menzies era, all schools were provided with science wings. In 1974, the Whitlam government decided that tertiary education would be free, and the Hawke government considered 'brain-based industries' to be of ever-increasing economic significance. The quest for Australia to become the 'clever country' had begun. As a result, Victorian high schools and technical schools were merged.

Falling Standards

Government control over children, via the school curriculum, reached its peak in 2008, when Australian State and Territory Education Ministers agreed on a 10-year education agenda known as the *Melbourne Declaration on Educational Goals for Young Australians*. Schools would now be involved in the intellectual, physical, social, emotional, moral, spiritual and aesthetic lives of all Australian children. The Australian Curriculum Assessment and Reporting Authority

(ACARA) developed the national curriculum and NAPLAN as part of this agreement.

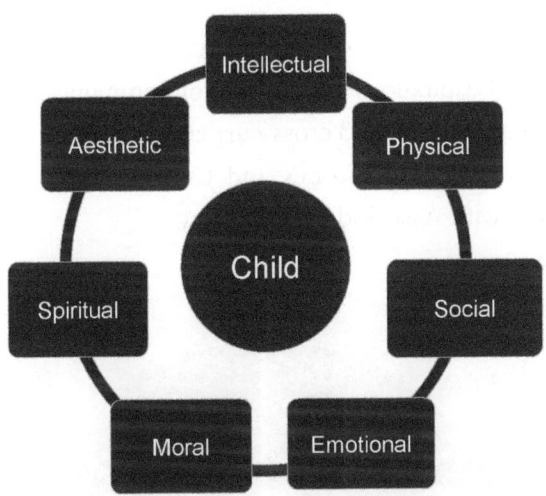

Diagram 8A: Melbourne Declaration Of Educational Goals For Young Australians

Two years prior to this agreement and its implementation, Australia had ranked among the top 10 countries in educational outcomes for 15-year-olds – in Science, Reading and Maths *(PISA 2006)*.

In 2015, seven years after the agreement, Australia's position had dropped to 10th in Science, 12th in Reading, and 20th in Maths. In 2017, according to United Nations Children's Fund *(UNICEF)*, Australia ranked 39th out of 41 countries for quality education.

Developing Local Curriculum

Adapted slightly for its own schools, the Victorian curriculum includes broad written statements that describe what students should know, understand, and be able to do, by the end of each *year level*. This is referred to as the 'standard curriculum.' Included in this standard are 9 learning areas, 7 general capabilities and 3 cross-curricular priorities.

Schools must decide on the curriculum they offer, based on the needs and aspirations of the school community. Their choices, however, must include the 3 cross-curricular priorities: Aboriginal and Torres Strait Islander Histories and Cultures; Asia and Australia's Engagement with Asia; and Sustainability.

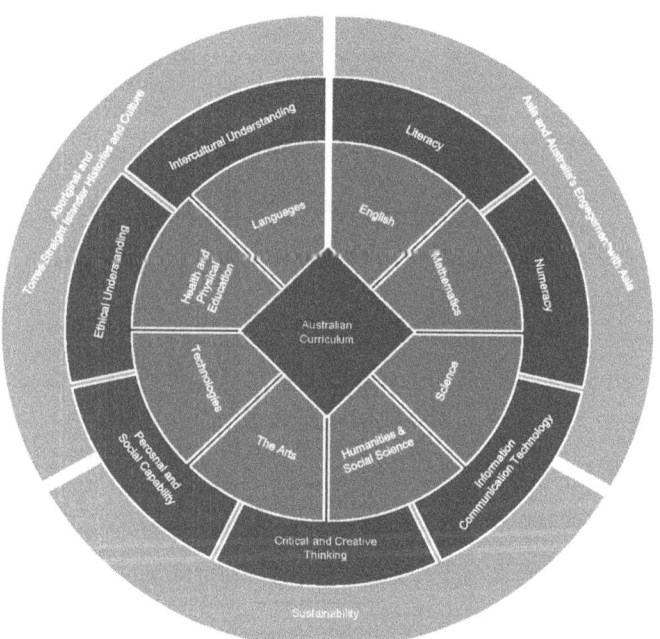

Diagram 8B: Australian Curriculum

The contradiction between allowing decisions to be made at the local school level and demanding the inclusion of cross-curricula priorities negates the guarantee of a standard curriculum and compromises what could be powerful opportunities at the local level.

Making the Grade

Subtle changes in language are perhaps not so subtle. Succeeding at a grade level traditionally meant a student had reached the required academic standard. A student who failed to reach the standard spent another year in that grade. On the other hand, if a student demonstrated capabilities beyond the standard, there was the opportunity to move up a grade.

Today grades have been replaced with years and the certificate for achieving a particular *standard of education* in reading, writing and arithmetic has been replaced with a national assessment that enables students to progress from one school year to next, regardless of the academic standard reached.

The Standard Framework

The framework for Australia's national system of education was designed to afford combined literary and moral instruction, separately from religious instruction. Over time, this framework has been tampered with, to the point where the provision of a standard curriculum has been compromised by an increase in content without an increase in hours, quality teaching or measures of teacher performance.

A Stable Australian Curriculum

As life goes on new chapters are added to the history books and, more specifically, to those chronicling Western Civilization. Even though attempts have been made to promote inaccurate interpretations, the events of the past cannot be changed. The same is true for fundamental aspects of the English language and Mathematics, and for the physiology of the human body.

Teaching methods change and ideas and concepts evolve. Words and meanings evolve, too, but the English language still has 26 symbols or letters, whose purpose is to create meaning on the page, through accurate representation of a writer's intended message, and to form words used in verbal communication. The numerical system is also based on symbols, and relies on the 10 digits from zero to nine. Without a fundamental understanding of these concepts, more complex application of the letters and numerals is not possible. Health and physical education promotes health and lifelong physical activity. Gymnastics or movement is the fundamental element of all sports.

Methodologies, philosophies and concepts will always evolve. There must, however, be a rich and stable framework that does not change. English, Mathematics, Health and Physical Education and a study of Western Civilization can be the basis of a stable Australian curriculum.

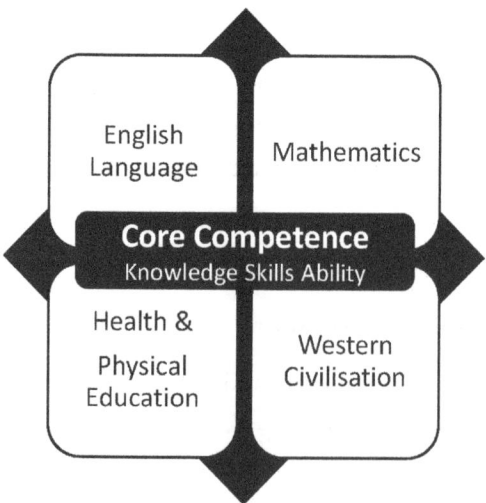

Diagram 8C: Fundamentals Of Stable Curriculum

Reduction of the current Australian curriculum, to a nationally agreed stable curriculum, would reduce the pressure on State and Territory governments to be the provider of all things education, and would invite the redistribution of funds from other portfolios into the education space.

Problem

There is no stable curriculum that requires teachers and students to meet a particular standard.

Consequences

- There is no longer an agreed standard of reading, writing and arithmetic.
- Assessment of English and Mathematics is not compulsory.
- Children can opt-out of assessments.
- Students are entering university and the workforce without an agreed minimum standard of English and Mathematics.

Key Solution

National level of English language, mathematics, health and physical education, Western Civilization – Inspectorate monitored.

Other Possible Solutions

- Mandate a national stable curriculum, including a Year 8 Certificate of Attainment, to be provided by the government, combined with electives at the local school level, to be paid for by parents and subsidised by government.

- The national stable curriculum will include English and Mathematics, Health and Physical Education and Western Civilization

- Perceptual Motor Program for P to 1 students for 30 minutes per day.

- Introduce different strands of English study, beyond the Year 8 certificate

Principle 9:

Clear Boundaries with Flexible Frontiers

In the end it never really changes – the human being will always need and desire change.

The year was 1979. Schools were still running on a 3-term cycle and I was in Form 4, the equivalent of today's Year 10. I had selected Community Involvement as my elective, and Tuesday afternoons were the highlight of the week. In Term 1 I visited the home of a family with pre-school children, and my task was to spend time with the children, giving respite to the mother. In Term 2 I went to see an elderly lady, Mrs Bird. We'd have afternoon tea and share stories of family, and she would tell me about her life during the war. Term 3 was spent at Heidelberg Special School, where I worked with children who had Down's syndrome. The positive impact of those experiences still remains with me.

The ultimate aim of education is freedom, belonging and responsibility. This is possible when there is a balance between control and flexibility. Our current education system is out of balance. Compulsory education is controlled by a bureaucracy that has a monopoly on teaching – when and how it happens, and by whom.

It hasn't always been this way.

In 1853, a report of the Civil Service of the Colony of Victoria presented the view that civil service should be of high reward, and high reward should be reserved for efficient service. Any compromise in the recruitment of those invited to serve the public would come at a profound cost to the country. The fewer people employed by the government, the better chance of recruiting the very best.

Decentralisation

Decentralisation in education describes the process of delegating or devolving authority to local schools. Suggested areas for decentralising bureaucracy are: administration; finance; and curriculum planning. It is fair to say, that if we accept this as the gold standard of decentralisation, Victorian schools are already there. Fundamental changes to the operational administration of the Department of Education, and an accountability framework for schooling have been in place for many years.

Schools are responsible for formulating their own policies, and recording family data in a centralised computer system known as CASES2. There are also selection panels for principals' appointments and promotions, and school councils have the authority to raise funds and distribute them as they see fit.

In real terms, these are superficial responsibilities, and although they appear to offer schools greater autonomy, they place schools in a compromising position. School councils are pseudo managers; they still have no control over the 'hiring and firing' of teachers. The department has determined all children are entitled to be enrolled in mainstream schools, and bind all schools to the bureaucracy by imposing the same curriculum – with the subtle option of adaptation to the local community.

Instruction and Education

Compulsory schooling provides buildings and staff for the provision of instruction. The instruction provided at school must contribute to a child's overall education.

Consider these four levels of education – craft, skill, trade and profession:

1. To have a craft is to demonstrate a competency – generally using your hands.

2. A skill is acquired through making deliberate and sustained efforts to carry out complex tasks.

3. Competency in a trade requires special training in manual work.

4. To have a profession, you must have acquired mastery of complex knowledge and skills, through study and practical experience, over a sustained period of time.

Each of these levels represent different ways of acquiring education. School is not the answer to all questions related to learning and teaching, particularly at the compulsory school age. It must be just one of a number of avenues that lead to the acquisition of education.

The Stable Curriculum

A craft expert, a skilled labourer, a tradesperson and a professional will each have varying degrees of competency; competency grows, however, from a standard that must be reached in reading, writing and arithmetic.

A stable Australian curriculum including English, Mathematics,

Health and Physical Education and Citizenship should be the only standard curriculum provided free of charge and it must be consistent across the nation. A regime of inspection would guarantee this stability, support accountability and ensure a clear boundary between certification of the standard to be achieved and recognition of achievement reached through other educational services.

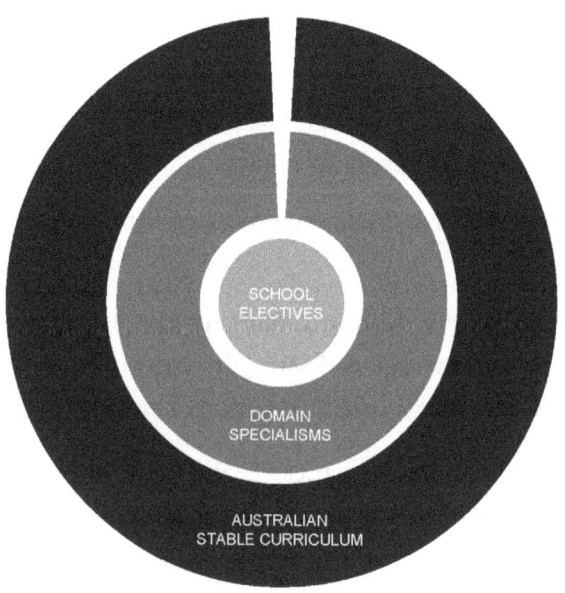

Diagram 9: Knowledge, Skills And Capabilities Distribution

Curriculum Specialism

As part of implied school autonomy, the Department of Education has determined that schools can decide on the learning programs they offer, based on the needs and aspirations of the communities they serve.

Some Victorian schools have been built and staffed for this specific purpose. The John Monash Science School and the Victorian College of the Arts are two examples.

Every school should have the opportunity to determine its curriculum specialisms, or to select from a generalist curriculum offered those offerings that would complement the stable curriculum.

Community Electives

Nothing should prevent State school buildings from being used for any purpose, on days and at hours when they are not used for secular instruction.

The introduction of electives, delivered by members of the wider community and delivered in school buildings or offered off-site, would:

- Broaden and diversify the scope of curriculum on offer
- Make provision for distinguishing between crafts, skills, trades and professions
- Connect students to the wider community

A consultative committee made up of public, commercial and industrial representatives would ensure local schools are driven by local community needs and offerings.

Problem

The bureaucracy has a monopoly on families with children of compulsory school age.

Consequences

- Central decisions affect all families with children of compulsory school age.
- Poor decisions have statewide consequences.
- Children are disengaged, particularly during early secondary school, with removal of the broader curriculum

Key Solution

Tiered curriculum at National, State and Local Level.

Other Possible Solutions

- A tiered curriculum, offered by a range of service providers.
- The central school would take responsibility for a stable curriculum.
- Other offerings agreed at local level.
- A local authority established to agree on school electives.

Principle 10:

Honour Discipline and Freedom Follows

The pathway to personal freedom is discipline.

Mark uses public transport twice every day to commute between home and work. One morning an elderly gentleman got on the tram. There was standing room only. A young boy immediately offered his seat to the elderly gentleman. The boy was immaculately dressed in school uniform – shoes shiny, tie perfectly knotted – and his hair was brushed and worn at a respectable length. He represented his school well, and Mark could sense the boy's pride and self-worth.

Two stops later, a group of boys got on the same tram. They were loud and obnoxious. Their shoes were scruffy, their ties undone and their shirts hanging out. As soon as a seat became available, they were the first to grab it before any adult standing had a chance. It was evident to Mark that their school had a very different philosophy.

Victoria Police was established in 1853. The establishment of schools and compulsory schooling came some 20 years later. It has been said that compulsory education was made law to prevent child labour and combat lawlessness among youth.

In reality, compulsory education encouraged families to think about the future of their children. It ensured an otherwise unaffordable education, more choice, greater responsibility and a stronger connection to the wider community. Education offered discipline, and freedom from poverty and lawlessness.

Youth Development

Today, many of our youth experience frustration, lack of self-worth and no sense of belonging. These feelings often lead to truancy, suspension and expulsion. The prevalence of bullying, widespread drug abuse and, sadly, suicide are extreme manifestations of youth disengagement and loneliness.

With no intention of offending those living with genuine cases, it has to be said that inappropriate behaviour or misconduct can also be hidden in the disability framework, under the guise of autism. It's a financial boon for some families and schools.

In a broader sense, political correctness means nothing can be said, for fear of offending someone. The tragedy of political correctness is not that it interferes with the freedoms of others, but that it is, in itself, discriminatory – particularly against males from western cultures. Statistically, among male youths there are higher incidences of truancy, expulsion, drugs, suicide, and antisocial behaviour, including involvement with gangs.

Youth development initiatives are healthy and promising alternatives to a life of disengagement, gang culture and crime. It provides a disciplinary foundation on which to rebuild self-worth, so youth can move forward and develop leadership skills.

Youth engagement initiatives include the cub and scout movement, St John Ambulance, camps conducted by Lions and Lord Somers and other not-for-profits. Through youth engagement initiatives, the disadvantaged or disengaged, can regain their dignity through discipline and the freedom that follows. They can experience a sense of community, promise for the future, and a life worth living.

Truancy

Truancy means the intentional, unauthorised absence from compulsory education. The Latin meaning of the word truant, however, is a vagabond or a person who wanders about with no settled home or job.

Reports of school absence, and, more important, an accurate distinction between truancy and absenteeism are not entirely clear. However, 2017 statistics provide some very telling scenarios. Students in Victorian government schools missed 1.5 million days for family vacations and a total of 10.6 million days overall. That's an average of 17 days for each student. Averages, however, do little to explain the effects of genuine absenteeism or truancy.

Holidays and fines aside, regional areas lead the charge on absenteeism. Victoria's hotspot is the Central Goldfields, where Year 10, 11 and 12 students missed an average of 53, 48 and 50 days respectively. In short, the typical senior students missed one quarter of the school year.

More than $44 million has been invested in a Navigator program which aims to build partnerships between schools and community organisations to support the states most disengaged students.

The extent of absenteeism and truancy raises many doubts about the actual existence of compulsory education, and points to the often fragile relationship between home, school and community.

Just as important, these statistics refer to just one state, which by its own admission, has the highest school attendance rate in the country.

Statistics aside, discussion is warranted regarding legislation that enables governments to enforce fines on parents. The Victorian Education Act (1958) included provision that parents shall cause their children of school age to attend a State school on every school half-day in each week – for two hours before noon or for two hours after noon. This act was repealed in 2005 by the Labor government and replaced by The Education Training and Reform Act 2006 (Victoria). This act insists on compulsory attendance during the entire time the school is open for instruction. The act and subsequent amendments enable principals to approve non-attendance. Powers are also given to attendance officers to monitor absenteeism, issue warnings, infringement notices and fines. On paper the education department stands for no nonsense. At present the fine of $81 a day can be imposed on parents whose child was an unauthorised absentee. But no fine has yet to be handed out.

Suspension and Expulsion

Also in 2017, 285 students were permanently removed from State government schools. The amount of funding for their re-engagement with education, and the cost to parents of alternative schooling are unknown. Figures related to school suspensions are also unknown.

What is clear, however, is that all students deserve to have a safe and positive learning experience, where they are engaged and supported to reach their full potential. Suspending students gives respite to other students and teachers but has an overall negative impact on everyone.

Shifting the Problem

Excluding students from school, including suspending them, shifts the problem from the school to the community. Unsupervised children are free to engage in dangerous and illegal activity, including theft, involvement with drugs and violent behaviour. The community must carry policing, medical and other costs.

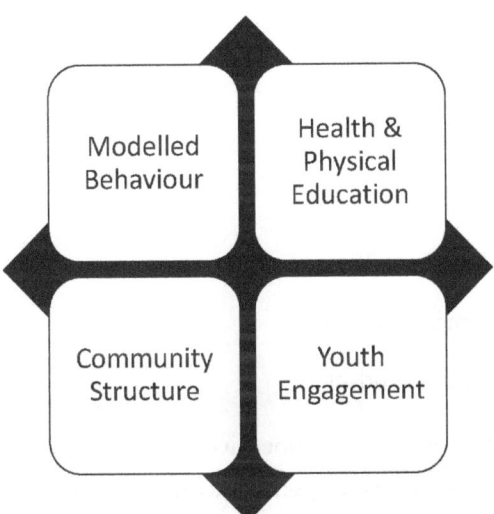

Diagram 10: Responsibility And Belonging

Modelled Behaviour

Schools have a duty of care to all students as soon as they come in through the school gates. This includes making sure students follow discipline procedures. When teachers have a poor dress code, and allow students to address them by their given name, and when students have the freedom to wear casual clothing, and may opt out of suspension, this works against a school's high expectations of behaviour.

Health and Physical Education

Students are expected to provide compulsory physical education of between 2.5 hours and 3 hours per week. Competitive sport is not compulsory. The benefits, however, include:

- Resilience
- Discipline
- Teamwork
- Fitness
- Leadership skills
- Time management
- A success mindset

Other advantages of competitive sport include extended use of school premises, social engagement with peers outside the mainstream school, and the opportunity to mix with other adults – particularly useful for boys, considering 75% of the teaching workforce is female.

Community Structure

Currently there are four law enforcement regions in Victoria: Northwest Metro; Southern Metro; Eastern; and West – each led by an Assistant Commissioner. Within the four regions there are 21 divisions, each with a superintendent. In each of the 21 divisions, there are 54 police service areas, with their local area commanders, or inspectors. The regional boundaries correspond with those of other Victorian government departments; this enables a cross-department service delivery, particularly during emergency management.

The challenge we currently face in Victoria is that our school regions and their subsets are not aligned. If we were to align the structure of schooling in Victoria with law enforcement and emergency services, schools would have a linked police station for any problems that might arise. Police and emergency service could better monitor schools, truants, families in general, and the community at large.

Discipline underpins every aspect of school life and is a key indicator of a successful school.

The problem:

Schools lack discipline and have the power to deny families their services.

The Consequences:

- Schools are not held to account for truancy, expulsion or suspension.
- Parents are held to account for child behaviour.
- There are costs to the community and other portfolios for poor discipline.
- Alternative curriculums and philosophy are not readily available in State schools.

Key Solution:

Marry schools and their communities with a similar structure to State law enforcement agencies.

Other Possible Solutions:

- Introduce compulsory sport as a component of the Australian Stable Curriculum

- Introduce compulsory school uniforms and dress codes in all State schools.

- Redistribute government funding and grants to the expansion of Youth Development initiatives.

Principle 11:

Forget Partnerships – Nurture Genuine Relationships

Children hold many titles including that of a student.

Most public school principals, teachers and employees belong to unions. The implied value of membership is that the legal duties of unions – bargaining for wages and benefits, and providing representation in the event of workplace grievances – are performed fairly for all members. Nothing could be further from the truth.

By its own admission, the Union has a global agenda and has strategically merged its various divisions to this end. In 1993 the Australian Capital Territory Union (ACTU) began to act on its policy to turn its 300+ unions into 20 or fewer 'super unions'. The Australian Teachers Union (ATU) became the Australian Education Union (AEU), and now anyone connected with 'education' falls under its membership umbrella.

The libertarian value of schooling is not connected with political motivation or religion. It is about responsible citizenship, choice, enterprise, personal satisfaction and consequence.

Schools are renowned for promising to be partners in the education of children of compulsory school age. Constitutionally, State governments are responsible for education. The only provisions they must make are facilities and employees to deliver standard instruction. Education Acts and Regulations and Ministerial Orders provide the detail with regard to the delivery of facilities and staff.

One-sided Benefits

In exchange for providing the standard curriculum, government employed teachers enjoy benefits that parents and students do not enjoy. Some examples are:

- Representation by a union.
- Representation by their employer – the State government of the day.
- A central bureaucracy of support, including lawyers, psychologists, etc.

Representation of Employees

The relationship between the Department of Education and its employees falls under the jurisdiction of unions, in Victoria, it is the Australian Education Union. Negotiations of any and all working conditions for teachers influence the provision of standard instruction. In every action taken by a teacher, the union has influence.

In fact, there is now virtually no point at which unions believe they should not, cannot, or do not involve themselves in matters of instruction.

Enterprise Agreements

Enterprise Agreements made on behalf of teaching staff are perceived to be in their best interests and, by default the students' best interests. Reduction in class size, for example, designed to reduce the workload and stress of teachers, is also intended to benefit students, in that they will receive more individual instruction from the teacher.

Reduction of class size, however, results in the need for additional employees and additional facilities. This benefits the union movement, in terms of additional memberships and more government investment in the building industry.

Biased Political Alliance

Unions are affiliated with the Labor movement. Representation of teachers and negotiation of working conditions could be considered as strategic activities favouring the Labor movement. When each workplace has a union representative, and that representative is granted special working conditions, including 8 days per year to attend union meetings, an obvious question arises: for whom is the union genuinely negotiating? Parents and students are directly affected by any and all negotiations but do they enjoy the benefits?

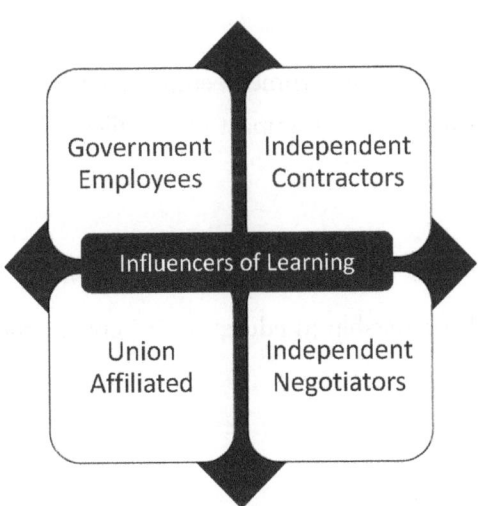

Diagram 11: Influencers Of Learning
The Compulsory School Years

Misrepresentation for Industrial Power

Poor representation has an impact as well. Principals and teachers, by their own admission, accept woeful working conditions. Unions have determined that teaching the standard curriculum can be achieved in no more than 22.5 hours face-to-face teaching. However, 80% of teachers allegedly work an average of 53 hours per week – that means unpaid overtime of 15 hours. When the number of hours is calculated, across a calendar year, it paints a picture intended to raise sympathy for overworked teachers, and to generate the acceptance of holidays as 'a hard earned break'. Like most other employees, teachers are entitled to 4 weeks of annual leave. If unions negotiated for a smaller curriculum, and a reduction in non-teaching responsibilities, student and teacher workloads would be less onerous. There would be no justification for teachers to take the same amount of leave as students do. When there is no fair and just negotiation for teachers, students and families carry the burden of schooling encroaching on their personal time.

Whatever affects Government employed teachers also involves unions; ultimately it has an impact on families. There is no genuine partnership.

Key Problem:

The only real partnership in education is between the State and the unions.

Key Solution:

Schools can employ from a State government pool or independent teachers not affiliated with the teacher's union.

Principle 12:

Home – The First Priority

The University of life is noisy, just as it should be.

A not-for-profit organisation works diligently to assist young girls who have left State care. Most of the girls have lived in multiple foster families and, as a result, have been enrolled in multiple government schools across the State. Until recently, schools have not been required to pass on student records from one school to another, when transfers occurred. Each time the girls began at a new school, a new record would be created.

Added to this, many of these foster girls have gone through compulsory schooling without a record of birth. There is no evidence that they are 18 years of age – the age at which the onus of duty of care is no longer on the State; some could, in fact, still be of compulsory school age. The Department of Education had no regard for their ongoing education or their whereabouts.

The non-transfer of records has not been limited to these girls. Cross portfolio and Education Department influence on the life of compulsory school age children, and their families, should be a measure of genuine service. It turns out that the family and the child are at the bottom of the 'care' chain.

Parents have every right to understand all that relates to schooling. Teachers have the right, and the freedom, to foster their own educational philosophy conditional that it doesn't contradict community agreement.

State VS Parent

Philosophies of learning and teaching have been celebrated, challenged and emulated for centuries. In about 380BC, Plato wrote *The Republic*, a dialogue that included his thoughts on the ideal society and the education of children. In his writing, he rejects the family unit in favour of *'guardians'*.

He reasoned that it would avoid nepotism and the amassing of private wealth. More importantly, he argued that children were the responsibility of the State, and no parent should know his own child, nor any child his parents.

Some educational and political leaders share Plato's sentiments. They hold the view that schools are the most appropriate places to equip children and youth with all the knowledge and skills required for living a fulfilling life.

Authentic leaders, on the other hand, believe that family is the bedrock of society and that education is the primary responsibility of the child's parents. They believe there must be transparency of government, and the provision of choice for parents – including a hand up for those with fewer choices than others. This puts the family first, with the school as the support service. This is an authentic school system.

To Feed One's Child

During World War II, just over 1500 teachers left the Department of Victoria to join the defence forces. Life in Victoria had to go on. Children still required instruction. Many temporary teachers were employed, most of whom were married women. At the end of the war, most of the married women resigned.

Teachers returning from service enthusiastically participated in a Reconstruction Training Scheme established by the Commonwealth Government. They undertook courses at Teachers' Colleges, senior technical schools or the University of Melbourne. Some teachers who chose to return to work immediately, were given short periods of refresher training before taking up duties in classrooms. Commonwealth and State governments worked diligently to support the return to civil life and to encourage those with a commitment to school education to perform their duties well.

With an increase in population, and recognition of the value of receiving a sound education, it was agreed in 1956 that secondary schooling should be made available for all. This gave rise to governments introducing bursaries and other incentives to attract more young graduates to a career in teaching. Job security and the guarantee of providing for a family have been used as magnets in the industry. These are still relevant issues that are part of enterprise agreements - negotiations between unions and the government.

Today, more than 75% of teachers are female. Their attraction to teaching has not only been about career choice, but also lifestyle choice. The family benefits when employment is secure. All things considered, teachers who have families are well looked after by government. Of more concern is that appeasement comes as part of the package. After all, who would take unnecessary risks with the security of one's own family.

Family as Client

Schools would not exist if not for the family unit. Service provided by a school is service provided to the family. A school's decisions and actions can affect a family for life. The family is the client. School employees are also members of families.

If the purpose of schooling – to belong, to be responsible and to work toward personal fulfilment – is not achieved, the consequences largely rest on the shoulder of the client. Schools are not compelled to provide a service until all students achieve the expected level of education. Students are not expected to attend school beyond the age of 17. The fallout of what does or does not take place during those compulsory years of school rests mainly with the client's family. The service provider remains employed, regardless of the service provided.

Home Across Portfolios

Education is the number one factor taken into consideration when dealing with issues related to the family, and every portfolio is affected by this understanding. Health, violence, employment, innovation and law and order, to name a few, refer to education to improve the lives of families. There is heavy expectation placed on education, and schools to carry a part of it. In many instances this makes good sense. In other instances, there can be consequences for teachers, students and their families, when educational expectations exceed what schools can provide.

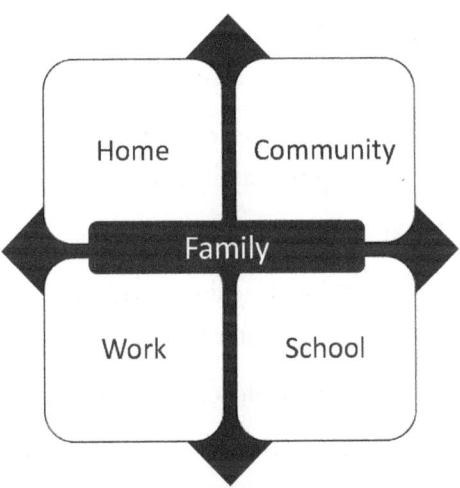

Diagram 12: School Influence In Perspective

It is true that education is key to eradicating many of society's problems. It is a matter for concern, though, that schools are considered the place for investment in prevention, intervention or innovation. The family is the fundamental group unit of society. The needs of the families as they support their children can be met across a range of portfolios better than they can within the constraints of only one portfolio: education. Families should be able to access the services of education providers outside the school and beyond compulsory school age. An extension of this idea would be for schools to join up, review and analyse available services and clients.

Key Problem:

Competing loyalties compromise the intended purpose of libertarian free schooling.

Consequences:

- Government employees in secure positions will not risk their own families to improve a failing school or system.
- School programs are developed to deal with issues and problems affecting the family and the home.
- The real cost of failed school programs cannot be measured
- Attracting people into teaching means families of State school employees are given greater benefits than average families
- Job security takes precedence over service provision
- There is no refund or second chance if a school fails a family.

Key Solution:

Use database to 'Join Up' relevant services to meet client's needs.

Other Possible Solutions:

- A pathway or plan of study leading to a qualification.
- Completion of VCE has no end date.

Principle 13:

Lead Schools by Working Beside Families

Schools would not exist if not for the family unit.

Jackie has been a school leader for more than a decade. She currently holds the position of principal in a regional primary school that has an enrolment of just over 400 children. Her primary responsibility is to lead the school in the education of all enrolled children. Four children, all from the same family, have recently been placed in foster care. As an advocate for these four children and their parents, Jackie is currently spending a great deal of time preparing for a court case.

She has described her position as untenable. She must provide support for this one family, while at the same time attempt to juggle her many other responsibilities. Some members of her teaching staff are fiercely passionate and capable professionals; the majority, however, are complacent, lazy and incompetent. The department expects her, as principal, to increase their capacity and improve their poor performance. She must also deal with school bureaucracy – the paperwork, surveys, policies and meetings. Added to that are the maintenance of the school buildings and grounds, and the management of school budgets.

All of these tasks take time away from what she loves most: being an instructional leader. Jackie went into the teaching profession to be an educator. Now, after ten years in a leadership role, she is a paper shuffling bureaucrat, pseudo site manager, social worker, administrator, accountant and policy maker.

She has done no further study, and her degree qualifications remain those of a generalist classroom teacher.

School leadership sits at the centre of a complex web of relationships that determine whether a community, or society, flourishes or fails. Like politicians, public school leaders have power and influence. They must not be swayed by political trends. They must remain impartial. Their role is to represent the hopes and dreams of the families they serve.

The power they have is extraordinary. They determine and lead the direction of the school, oversee facilities, lead teaching and learning, and are responsible for the investment of State and Federal government and non-government financial contributions. They hold information on families, and can involve themselves in every area of the life of the family.

Principals have also been blessed with a small window of entitlement that carries more weight than the love of any parent. *Parens patriae* is Latin for parent of the nation. In law, it refers to the power of the State to intervene and act as the parent of a child, where there is parental neglect. Based on State mandates, it effectively gives a school or its representative, the principal, the right to make decisions, or it hands children decision making powers, without the consent of their parents. These decisions can affect the life of a family forever.

A Principal's Qualifications

Every school is run like a small business. Although there are general similarities among schools, each individual school has its own clientele and employees, and provides its own services. Relationships between the school and its community, including its employees, are influenced by the culture created by the school leader – the principal. You could say that the principal is the key influencer in the life of a school.

Despite their influence, teachers are not required to undergo any formal qualification to secure the position of Principal. Professional development courses are available, including, for instance, government run courses provided by Victoria's Bastow Institute.

Taking on other leadership roles, including that of Assistant Principal, is the most common pathway to a principal's position. Teachers aspiring to leadership roles are often taught and mentored, on the job, by the serving principal. In these cases, the competency of the current principal influences the future capabilities of the aspiring principal.

In real terms, 17-year-old students could make the transition from school student to university student and then move back into schools as teachers and then as principals with no need for further study or experience beyond that involved in completing a teaching degree. No formal certification to achieve the status of principal is required. In such cases, their workplace experience is limited to being permanent daytime residents of educational institutions. And this is the only view they bring to the role of principal. Principals usually come directly from a bank of government employees. Leaders in other industries, who do not have a teaching background, do not apply.

A Principal's Workload

For some principals, daily working life can be extremely demanding and, at times, overwhelming. For others, not so much. Some might continue their studies – for example working towards a PhD – while maintaining a full-time workload. By and large though it's the diverse nature of a principal's role that can be the most challenging.

Unions have long fought for better working conditions for principals. A recent survey of principals indicated that more than 85% of principals want an increased budget, less red tape, better qualified staff – particularly in the area of wellbeing – and more administrative support. More than 70% of principals want the power to hire and fire. Bigger budgets, smaller class sizes and increased wages will not solve all the problems. What's needed is systemic reform in the process of determining who leads schools.

Conflict of Interest

Teachers go in to the workforce for two main reasons: they have a genuine commitment to teaching and making a difference in the lives of children, or they see it as a lifestyle choice. Principals come from both of those pools.

Principals must manage complex social issues and must have the relevant skills to do it. An understanding of human nature is paramount if one is to lead a school. Herein lies the dilemma. People skills aren't enough. For every decision a principal must make, there are conflicting loyalties: to the government that the principal represents; to the service the school provides; and to the client-family. Not everyone wins.

The principal's own interests also come into play. Schools are in the business of providing a service – education – but a principal with a passion for educational leadership, for example, will lead a school in a very different way from one whose interests lean more towards administration.

Privacy, Capability, Diversity

The legal implications associated with duty of care can compromise principals. At the simplest level, compulsory attendance gives a principal a window into the life of a family. Student absences must be noted and principals have the right to deny a request for planned absence if they feel the reasons are unsuitable. The principal, on behalf of the government, can monitor the family life of every child of compulsory school age. In more sensitive cases, including those involving child custody, principals are privy to the details of family life. The personal life of one family can involve an inordinate amount of a principal's time, and take precedence over educational leadership.

Small and medium business owners do not concern themselves with the personal details of their clients. They concern themselves only with the issues that affect their ability to deliver the promised service. People are employed with qualifications or specific skill sets, either as staff or sub-contractors, enabling service providers to focus on their craft. When the principal-owner spends more time on accounts, staffing and troubleshooting, and less time on client service, the business will eventually fall over. School principals should view themselves as business owners.

Principals lead organisations that provide the service of education. Principals must be instructional leaders. All other issues are secondary to this responsibility, and not all other issues are the business of the principal.

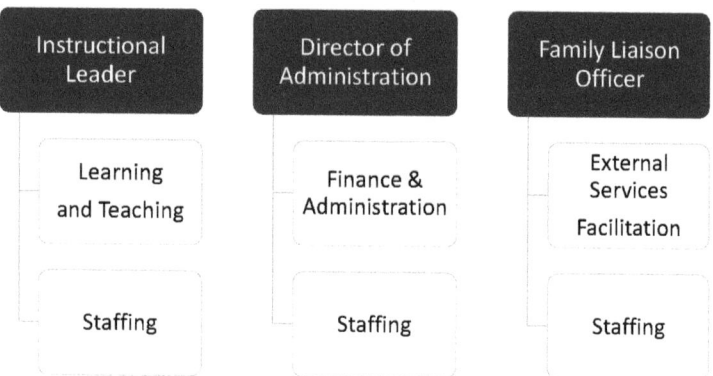

Diagram 13: Leadership Diversity

Key Problem:

School education is compromised by a Principal's diverse responsibilities and priorities.

Consequences:

- Under qualified individuals sometimes lead schools.
- Education is not a priority.
- Parents disclose personal information to strangers who work in schools.
- Unions do not address the real issue of principal workload or teacher incompetence.
- The lives of children depend on a principal's performance.

Key Solution:

3 Tiered Leadership model – Instructional Leader, Chief Executive Officer, Family Liaison Officer.

Other Possible Solutions:

- Instructional leaders take responsibility for matters of curriculum and assessment.
- Make *Masters of Educational Leadership* compulsory for becoming an Instructional Leader.
- Open school leadership positions to leaders of other industries.
- Place an Instructional Leader in every school. Small schools can share CEO and FLO positions.

Principle 14:

Pedagogy – The Heartbeat of Every Classroom

The primary choice is to be yourself. Everyone else is taken.

Simon and Annie worked in the same school. Annie taught in the lower primary area, and Simon in the senior primary. They had a profound respect for one another, and enjoyed comparing the strengths and limitations of their personalised teaching styles. After three years they agreed to team teach.

Their classroom comprised of 64 children. Making creative use of space and existing furniture they created two distinct learning and teaching spaces. The first was structured in a formal arrangement with rows of tables facing the front of the room. This was in keeping with Simon's preferred organisation. The other section was scattered with groups of tables, a mat, and shelving to create distinct areas. It was less formal, and based more on Annie's preferred approach. Both areas ensured teacher-directed learning with scope for child-centred arrangements so that students could apply core learning.

Simon and Annie had an extremely successful year. They learned from one another, and applied each other's suite of teaching methodologies to suit the many different in-school and out-of-school experiences they offered their students.

To Teach

The word 'teacher' can be traced back to the Greek term *deiknumi*, which means 'to point out' or 'to show'. Many have said that to teach is an honour. This badge is best bestowed on the average teacher.

The finest of all teachers are knowing. They give of themselves freely, but do not give of themselves lightly – that would be arrogance. The finest of teachers know how and why another will benefit from their own life lessons. After all, how can one best teach another, without having been in that same or similar position first?

All of life's lessons are connected to the human spirit. Every challenge, interaction, failure and achievement is intertwined with the lessons we must learn to become human, to find inner peace. To teach or to point out issues of ethics, spirituality, wisdom, faith, politics and tradition is not to point out a life of peace. To teach is to guide another human being to take one step closer to finding that peace for themselves. Like the great philosophers of centuries past, teachers must have knowing, if they are to be teachers of the highest order.

Pedagogy

In professional circles, teaching is often better known as pedagogy. A simple definition of pedagogy is 'the art and science of teaching'.

All teachers have their own unique pedagogy or 'DNA'. In other words, every teacher has an individual and unique approach or methodology to choosing and delivering the curriculum – that is, what is intended to be taught and learned.

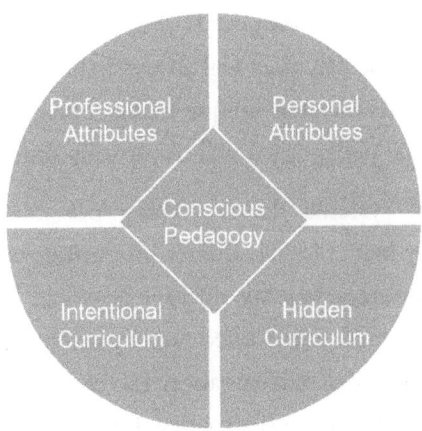

Diagram 14A: Teacher Autonomy And Professionalism

Pedagogy is influenced by many factors. Personal attributes – including communication skills, productivity, motivation and work ethic – influence the way teachers view students and the curriculum. Effective use of time, and the ability to adapt and think on one's feet are essential. An instrinsic understanding of precisely what must be learned within a given time frame influences the success or otherwise of a classroom.

The pinnacle feature of pedagogy is making choices about the curriculum. In other words, teachers are the ultimate masters of the curriculum universe. Personal life views, teaching strategies, relationships between students' parents and personal distractions influence a teacher's daily choices. What is written in a curriculum framework is rarely, if ever, delivered in the literal way it is intended. By and large, the greatest influences that affect student success are the pedagogical differences between teachers. In spite of that, teacher pedagogy and performance are not measured.

Measuring Pedagogy

Imagine if teachers were 'shapes'. If they persist in thinking they must be squares, that's the way they will always behave. They'll never get to see the finer points of their unique being. Their star qualities – their potential personal pedagogy – will never fully shine.

State school systems do everything possible to maintain the status quo. They like colorful squares, but cringe when a shining star appears. To encourage teacher difference would be to acknowledge that teaching is not like a well-oiled factory machine, but one requiring investment in personal performance. If that were to happen, there would be a clear need for performance measures, which might involve measuring the public servants who control other public servants. An uncomfortable idea. But, just as teachers measure student outcomes, teaching outcomes must also be measured.

Consider this figure: $249,420,000. That's almost one quarter of a billion dollars. This is the minimum figure spent on teacher professional development in Victoria in 2016. Don't confuse this spending with investment. It's not. Spending on professional development is often limited to system wide initiatives, at times worthwhile, in most, compromising professional accountability. There are no workshops on refining parent-teacher relationships, on shaving unnecessary content from the curriculum, on ethics and choices in content, or on time management. Professional development is not genuinely about investing in the teacher or the student. Since the 1970s it never really has been. It's about spending.

Teachers experience a combination of mandated and chosen professional development. If they were invited to own and develop their own pedagogy, and if they realised that their performance could be the difference between being employed or not, then the measurement of student outcomes would also take on a whole new meaning. Teacher performance will always affect student outcomes.

The Teaching Profession

A profession is a disciplined group of individuals who adhere to ethical standards and practice beyond the personal obligations or desires of an individual. A profession can define and demand high standards of behavior and service, and enforce them. The community benefits from these standards and knows when they are absent.

Teaching at present is not a profession. It can be – but only when over-decorated self-interest is expunged.

Certificates of Employment

More than 60% of small businesses close within their first three years. Between 40% and 50% of teachers leave the job after 5 years. Three key issues that affect small business failure also affect teaching. They are: cash flow; sudden rapid growth; and lack of knowledge.

1. Cash Flow

Small business is responsible for its cashflow. When it's missing the business goes under. This is a problem in teaching. Teachers are at the bottom of the financial table and have no control of cash flow. They sit at the cold face of service delivery, but have little or no connection to the cashflow used for the service they deliver.

2. Sudden Rapid Growth

Students who graduate from university have had some practical experience of school life. During their school placements, they observe, teach the occasional lesson and perhaps teach for a day, a week or several weeks in a row. They do so under supervision, with backup – another teacher, and that teacher's personal pedagogy. Pre-service teachers never have to disclose fully their capabilities and limitations. Then it's graduation and employment, and the newly fledged teacher must grow and adapt rapidly to deal with the complexities of the art and science of teaching. Some will excel; some will meander through the process; some won't survive.

3. Lack of Knowledge

Qualifications don't necessarily equate with capability. In terms of 'trained' teachers, this has, unfortunately, never been more true. If you went to a hairdresser you would expect to find someone who knew how to cut and style your hair. Similarly, you would regard it as necessary that your medical practitioner had the knowledge either to treat you or recommend you see someone more qualified. In schools, out-of-field teaching is commonplace. On a regular basis, teachers are asked to teach outside of their field of expertise. Pedagogy – the art and science of teaching – is greatly compromised. For the teacher, it's a matter of survival. For the student, who knows? 'There's always next year' – the standard unspoken understanding between teachers.

Transitions and Pathways: The Commitment Continuum

It's not uncommon for parents to place a high level of trust in teachers. It makes sense to assume that those who work with children possess immense knowledge, wisdom and integrity.

Good teachers know how to connect with an individual. They provide the right encouragement and challenges. They have high expectations that the learner be responsible, curious and innovative. They know the synergy between learning and teaching. They embrace their own pedagogy.

However, the teaching profession is no different from any other. Every school has its share of outstanding teachers, who take their job seriously and provide a service above and beyond expectations. And, as in any other profession, there are those with lesser degrees of capability or commitment.

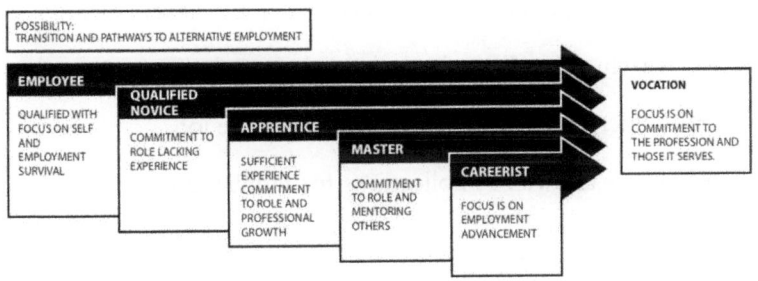

Diagram 14B: The Commitment Continuum

During their careers, teachers move along what I call the commitment continuum. Most teachers will be at different points on this continuum at various times in the course of their working lives. Some teachers will see that the passport to professional success is owning their own pedagogy. Sadly, some won't care. Measuring teacher performance in the workplace must ultimately be about measuring the value of the workforce and the value of transitioning out those who can be of service elsewhere.

Key Problem:

Teacher performance is not measured.

Consequences:

- Teachers are employed by the Department.
- Parents cannot select the person teaching their children.
- Principals cannot select staff to suit the philosophy of the school.
- Teachers cannot be fired.
- Job security takes precedence over job performance.
- Teaching is a lifestyle choice, not a profession.
- Underperforming colleagues stay in the job.
- There are wider implications for families and community.

Key Solution:

- Teachers present their pedagogy for quarterly review. Adjustments made in teaching, assessment and service providers.

Principle 15:

Child and Student Are Not Synonymous

A child is many things – 'student' being just one of them.

Gemma, as a student preparing for Year 10, was offered Year 11 Business to add to her course load. A few weeks later, she was advised that she would not be suitable for the class. Gemma's mother, Kate, requested a meeting with the year level co-ordinator and business studies teacher, to find out why the offer had been reversed. 'On reflection, Gemma won't be able to manage the content', the co-ordinator told her.

Kate asked how many businesses the co-ordinator and the teacher had owned and/or managed. The answer was 'None'. Kate informed the school staff that both she and her husband had owned and managed a number of businesses and, as Gemma had grown up, she had also participated in a variety of ways. Kate also made it clear that she and her husband would be happy to help Gemma with her studies, where necessary.

'Surely this would fully support Gemma in the subject?' Kate suggested.

'No', said the co-ordinator. 'We teach from this textbook. Gemma's experience and what you and your husband do don't really relate to this content'.

Kate did some further research, obtained external advice and took the matter to the school leadership. Gemma completed the Year 11 Business course, with excellent results.

The family is the fundamental unit of society. When schooling was formalised, it encouraged and enabled all children, regardless of class, to be educated. It was believed that compulsory schooling would provide opportunities for self-development, a sense of belonging and personal fulfilment, and responsible economic contributions to the wider community. It was a noble, exciting and egalitarian possibility. Since then, conflict over ideology has all but removed this vision and has instead placed a noose around the personal lives of children and their families.

The Case of Care or Control

In the United Kingdom, the outcome of a famous 1985 legal battle, known as the Gillick case, sent ripples through compulsory education and family life across the world. The key decision rejected the notion that children would remain under the control and authority of their parents (or other adult carers) until they reached legal age. It was determined that if children had the intelligence and understanding necessary to consider various possibilities, in order to make an informed decision, they must be able to do so. Some powers to protect and promote a child's welfare might be given to parents, but generally, powers of choice rested with the child.

A Student has More Value than a Child

Compulsory schooling affects children and their families for life. The majority of a child's life – 13 out of 18 years – is spent in compulsory schooling. The right of a school to exert a duty of care over the child as student, is clearly documented in legislation. Government mandates, the school's choice of classroom teachers, and decisions made at the central level for students, all weigh heavily on the life of a child. Parents are no longer the only carers and decision makers.

The unequivocal right of every child to receive an education comes with an implied partnership between parents and the State government. Compulsory attendance at a school controlled by a bureaucracy, and the legislation that protects it, makes it clear that the State government is the senior partner. The obligation on parents to ensure school attendance offers no real protection of a child's welfare, but it certainly guarantees the child's welfare remains in the hands of the State.

Open to Interpretation

Trying to interpret legislation, particularly definitions, can be rather difficult for those who don't have a law degree. Mandates given by the State are limited to the 'plain English' interpretations provided. Mandates are part of a web of Ministerial Orders and laws that enable schools to make decisions about children, because they also happen to be students. A simple example: 'Educators must have regard to the provision of opportunities for parents to participate in the education of their children'. The word 'must' might imply that parents have rights. However, on closer inspection, the statement can be interpreted to mean educators must only give it some thought.

Neither home nor school alone can raise or educate the whole child. The use of this terminology adds weight to the potential value for State control, via the school, over the total life of a child.

Teacher, Principal or Parent

The best interests and the education of a child extend beyond the family home and into the school grounds. Teachers, principals and parents have influence over that education. The State suggests its responsibility goes further – a responsibility for the best interests of the child and for the education of the 'whole child'. How can that be? A child is only a student while attending school. The boundary between 'student' and 'child' is not clear. The roles of parent, teacher and principal are not clear.

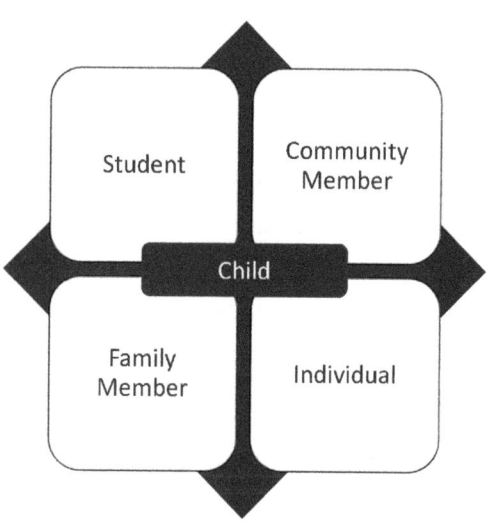

Diagram 15: The Roles Of A Child

Personal Lives

Family life is private. What takes place inside the family home is generally nobody else's business. Schools, however, gather information about families and are often privy to parents' personal lives. They can become gossip centres, where a family's details are openly discussed and children's health and academic records are openly displayed in staffrooms. The lives of children and their families become accessible to the public by the very nature that children also happen to be students.

On the other hand, parents are not privy to the personal lives of school employees. All parties have a duty of care to the child, but not all parties are bound by disclosure. Principals and teachers, as employees of the State, are protected from such exposure.

Schools provide instruction. They are not churches, health centres, dental practices, or family planning clinics. Some of these services, however, are offered in school buildings. In schools, it is logical for these services to be distributed among service providers. It is also logical for principals to have boundaries: they serve as instructional leaders for students. Assistance in other areas of a child's life, requested by or on behalf of parents, is better provided by professionals employed for the purpose. Schools are places of instruction. They are not homes or social service providers.

Key Problem:

Family life is entering the public domain.

Consequences:

- Family details are open to the public.
- School employees share information about families.
- Principals have control over the whole 'child', rather than the 'student'.

- Parents are not always the principle figures in their own child's life.

- The State can control the life of a child via the alleged provision of education, as opposed to compulsory schooling.

- Principals are distracted by family matters; this hampers their responsibility for student instruction.

Key Solution:

Family Liaison Officer (FLO) key communicator with family on matters of the 'child'.

Other Possible Solutions:

- Mediation specialists available across school regions; parents can access them with regard to personal family matters.

- Family Liaison Officer inform principals on matters pertaining to education only.

Principle 16:

Diversify Teacher Quality

Teacher professionalism is noticed, modelled, adapted and duplicated.

Nola began her teaching career as a mature age student. She attended Teacher's College in her 20s, with students who had just come out of secondary school. The diverse experiences she had, prior to entering the school system, were invaluable. The bureaucracy and its control over education, however, were immediately evident to her. The work ethic she brought from other work experience, and the questions she raised, posed a threat to colleagues who had only ever been students before they became teachers.

Over time, those who helped with her professional growth in education were not teachers; her mentors came from outside the bureaucracy and the classroom. Mature individuals with a wealth of experience in a variety of vocations provided her with a vastly different education from what she could gain from workshops or school-based promotions.

For centuries, parents have carefully chosen highly regarded individuals – including people of faith, philosophers, and the well-educated – to contribute to the education of their children. For Australia's first students, this included the wives of clergy and well educated convicts. The evolution of schooling, combined with the gold rushes, brought an influx of immigrants, creating a need for teachers beyond the carefully chosen.

Denominational schools were established in Melbourne, with contributions from the community and a some supplemented by public funds. A Denominational Schools Board was also established; its role included development of a code of regulations for the conduct and regulation of church schools receiving public funds. In 1848, Governor Charles La Trobe received a review from the Board. Of the 120 teachers employed, some were capable, but many were '*not worth even the paltry salaries they were receiving*'. Only five had been trained, and about a quarter had some experience as tutors. Inferior standards of teachers' spelling and handwriting were rife. Their particularly poor capabilities in arithmetic meant the subject was often omitted from instruction altogether. Substandard teacher performance in the fundamentals of reading, writing and arithmetic prompted the development of the public school sector.

Today, some parents still invest in subject-specific tutors, however, compulsory schooling replaced the parent as the direct employer, and the teacher has replaced the carefully chosen tutor. Bureaucracy plays a significant role in the life of the child and the family.

Out-of-field Teachers

The Australian Council of Education Research, established in 1930, is renowned globally for its work. The organisation's *Teacher Workforce in Australia: Supply, Demand and Data* report of 2015 identified 'out-of-field' teachers – those who teach beyond their qualification. Statistics from this report reveal the stark reality that many teachers fall into this category. History was once a valued feature of the standard curriculum; 75% of courses are now delivered by out-of-field teachers. The situation is similar for mathematics (20%) and geography (40%).

Justifications for out-of-field employment include class size and the need to place competent teachers with senior students to boost Year 12 results. Of greater concern is that schools succumb to the expectation that they will offer a diverse curriculum, regardless of school size, location or teacher capability.

State governments register schools to teach a standard curriculum. The absence of subject matter experts is deplorable. The clear message sent by the bureaucracy is that the State government concerns itself only with the provision of employees, not educators. This issue alone erases any and all rhetoric related to commitment to children's education. Clearly, no value is placed on a subject, its teachers, or the students who are interested in studying it.

Generalist Teachers

Primary school teachers, with generalist qualifications, can accept positions of employment to teach at any of eight different year levels, across every area of the curriculum – all of which have different demands in terms of complexity of knowledge, understanding and skills. Teachers can be asked to move across year levels at any time. They are not required to be appropriately capable, or sufficiently prepared for the move. It is acceptable for teachers to use periods of student non-attendance (8 weeks per year) for vacation, instead of for upskilling or reacquainting themselves with content expectations; this leaves the bureaucracy and the State government liable to a charge of negligence.

In 2008, every State and Territory agreed it to be absolutely necessary that schools be involved in intellectual, physical, social, emotional, moral, spiritual and aesthetic aspects of students' lives.

What arrogance, when the fundamental of education and subject expertise are not seen as having any value.

School Inspection

A vigilant and frequent inspection of schools has proved to be the best means to render schools more efficient. Regional inspectors, charged with monitoring teacher performance, curriculum and student outcomes once helped schools achieve educational credibility within the school sector and the wider community. Held in high regard, inspectors were well known across their community and were usually members of volunteer organisations including Rotary, Lions and the Freemasons.

School inspectors have been replaced by regional teams and a self-assessment model. Internal review, with no negative consequences for inaccuracy, has become the benchmark for potential improvement, which might or might not occur, once again without consequence.

Greater respect and responsibility for education, and the reintroduction of a genuine inspectorate would pave the way for accountability, vocational responsibility, and the return of teaching to its rightful place as a profession. The current self-assessment model is nothing more than a selfish attempt to promote self-importance.

Model and Other Pre-Service Schools

Melbourne's first National Model School was a co-educational boarding facility in East Melbourne. It provided courses for students who wanted to become educators. Its purpose was to ensure that civil servants responsible for delivery of instruction did so to the highest of standards. These schools later became Melbourne High School and Melbourne Girls High School.

New model schools, referred to as Teachers Colleges were later established throughout the State. Trainee teachers would specialise in areas such as Health and Physical Education or Infant Teaching and become highly qualified persons, possessing a thorough knowledge of the art of teaching. For capability beyond their initial fields of experience, teachers were required to do further study. Teaching was not taken for granted, and the level of capability involved was highly valued.

In 1964, *The Report of Tertiary Training in Australia* recommended that an autonomous Board of Teacher Education be established in each State, and charged with the authority to advise governments in relation to future developments in teaching training. Its view was that the educational experience of any child, gained from kindergarten to university, depended largely on the extent to which teachers were prepared to perform their tasks. A further recommendation was that the Board 'should also become the channel through which Commonwealth funds would be made available for the development and the preparation of teachers.

In reality, the interpretation of these recommendations saw the closure of all teachers colleges in Victoria; the university was to be sole provider of pre-service teacher education. The university was no longer the pre-eminent training ground for the professions, but was reimagined as a laboratory for the rewriting of history and the eradication of content expertise. The thread of political correctness has been woven into the fabric of every university degree. Teachers graduate from institutions that are very much the same in nature – with the same left-leaning ideologies, and the same levels of incompetence.

Four Levels of Capability

Consider these four levels of capability: craft, skill, trade and profession.

1. To have a **craft** is to demonstrate a competency – generally using your hands.

2. A **skill** is acquired through making deliberate and sustained efforts to carry out complex tasks.

3. Competency in a **trade** requires special training in manual work.

4. To have a **profession**, you must have acquired mastery of complex knowledge and skills, through study and practical experience, over a sustained period of time.

Each of these levels requires study, instruction and the relevant literature. In other words, these levels represent four different ways of acquiring education.

Victoria's curriculum, based on the Australian model, does not concern itself with, or distinguish between, these capabilities. The government, via the Australian Curriculum, has control over the depth of subject specialism.

The closure of technical schools, the demise of hand-eye co-ordinated subjects, and the increase of academic subjects, manipulated for political gain, have all compromised the value and potential contribution of every child of compulsory school age.

Certified to Teach

There is much to be learned from the past, from the interpretation of reform, and from the many recommendations governments have received. A return allowing children to study in the four levels of capability would require the introduction of a diverse study platform for which teachers would receive certification and be employed to deliver.

Diagram 16A: Flexible Work Practices – 15 years+

Specialist Teacher – 4-year degree

- In one of 4 stages of school certification
- Content specialism for stages 3 or 4
- Health and Physical Education
- One only diverse ability specialism (e.g. sight impaired or gymnastics)

Vocational Expert Teacher

- Teaching degree acquired after workplace experience in previous vocation.

Workplace Teacher

- Degree in Adult Education (inclusive of English and Mathematics) for on the job workplace education

Teacher Mentor

- Those aged over 55 – from fields of diverse expertise – for mentoring students, particularly in the soft / essentials skills

Pathways Teacher

- Degree in Career and Study Pathways
- Expert in transitions and pathways: cross-campus; workplace; youth engagement; study

Support Teacher

- Today's existing classroom teachers

Apprentice Teacher

- In-field intern at a 'common school' – a school accredited for on-the-job pre-service experience – who remained in association with the school and commenced employment there, on completion of a degree.

Imagine a world where the teacher would no longer be someone who had made the transition from 17-year-old school leaver to teacher, but a person with a genuine field of expertise – a professional.

No longer would schools be limited to having students teach children. Instead, children would be taught by adults with expertise, stories to tell, and wisdom to impart – all arising from their life-skills, capabilities and successes in their own field. The range of expertise would be broad, bold and beneficial to all.

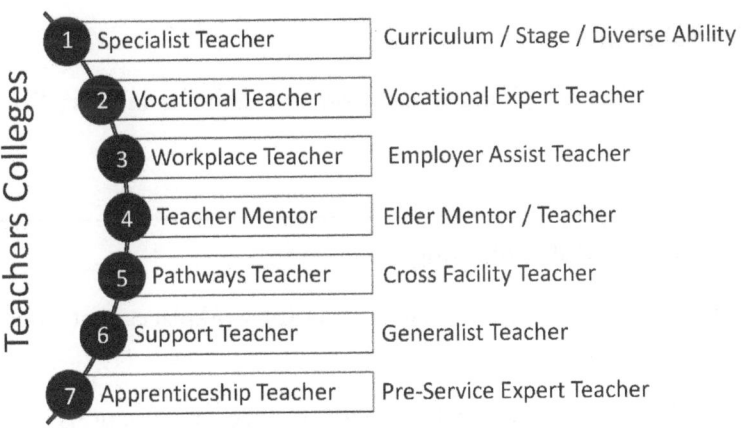

Diagram 16B: Purposeful Teaching

Key Problem:

Universities have a monopoly on education degrees and certification.

Consequences:

- Students of compulsory schooling become teachers of compulsory schooling.
- Four levels of capability are not valued.
- Left wing views and ideology are accepted and passed on without criticism; they feed the curriculum.
- Superficial coverage of disciplines has replaced depth of understanding and capability.
- Education has become a means to employment, not a major contribution to human wisdom.

Key Solution

Establish Teachers Colleges and Common Schools in every School Region.

Other Possible Solutions

- Establish Commonwealth grants for workplaces that offer schooling.
- Build local partnerships with service organisations for mentoring teachers.

Principle 17:

Negotiate on Merit

Our actions do not define us; they are part of our valuable life story.

Destruction by fire is devastating. When a State government primary school was destroyed, even though it was heart breaking for the community, such was the optimism of the school's highly regarded principal, she showed them it was 'a chance to promote growth through adversity, and convert a negative into a positive'. She was determined not to fail her community. Temporary accommodation nearby, in an unused and derelict State high school, marked the beginning of a journey that would bring the community even closer. Next came the school rebuild. It wasn't without its problems – including the challenges of dealing with the Department of Education – but the primary school was rebuilt and life moved on.

No-one could have foreseen further devastation on the horizon. The principal's tenure was coming to a close. The process for reappointment was progressing and then the unthinkable happened. Rumours about the principal began to circulate. The once close-knit community was thrown into turmoil. Many supported the principal's reinstatement; others stood firmly by the rumours. Tensions escalated, the Department of Education brought in security guards, and police attended on various occasions. Trespass notices were issued to parents who supported the principal, and the rumours continued. The Department of Education defended the rumours; the principal defended her reputation and paid all legal fees out of her own pocket. The case was settled in favour of the Department, and the principal lost her job, her reputation, her livelihood and her health. And, as if that weren't enough, her husband, who was a member of the school staff, was also removed. Two highly regarded educators, who had met while teaching in the 70s, were destroyed by the very school system to which they had devoted their working lives.

Principals are drivers of the vision, culture and results of their school. Not all principals, however, are leaders. School leadership requires a healthy combination of personal and professional qualities and capabilities. Top performing principals are those who understand the community and deliver on local community issues. Their salaries, however, do not always reflect their capabilities.

A principal's performance affects every government portfolio and every portfolio has an impact on a principal's performance. Curriculum, treasury, jobs and small business; social services, health and immigration, all play a role in the successes or failings, and the decisions made by a school leader. Performance must create value and that valued must be able to be measured. The measure of a principals' and teachers' performance is not based on the services provided, but on their clients – the students and their families; incremental pay increases occur regardless of performance.

The Client

Schools state that a focus on 'the whole child' is at the heart of their strategic direction. This focus includes the child's intellectual, physical, social, emotional, moral, spiritual and aesthetic development. It's a bold statement, implying that every teacher can meet the needs of every child. It isn't true. Every child is unique, and a child's development requires the support of many people. Children are also part of a larger network – their classmates.

On a day-to-day basis, children spend a great deal of time with their peers. Most time is spent participating in whole class or group experiences and less time in one-to-one interactions with their teacher. Despite the collective approach to instruction, children must be assessed on their own merit. There is no group NAPLAN assessment or group-based Year 12 certificates. The success or otherwise of a child's life at school is measured on the child's individual performance. A child's life choices are also influenced by a measure of individual performance. The same cannot be said for teachers.

The Service Provider

Teachers have the greatest in-school influence on student engagement and achievement. The effectiveness of the classroom teacher is critical to the effectiveness of the student's education. Like each child, every teacher is unique. Teachers bring their own pedagogical influences to school every day. Not all teachers have the same qualifications, level of skill, or range of teaching experience. They have their own way of delivering the curriculum and their own relationships with their students.

Teachers have a combined wealth of experience, wisdom and talent. Each brings a unique personality, loyalty, ambition, and commitment to the role. Some are generalist teachers with natural talents in specialist areas; others are qualified specialists in their own right.

Their performance and pay, however, are not measured by their talents, commitment or outcomes achieved. It is assumed that by virtue of their being employed, their performance has merit, and is equitable to that of their peers. Reward for their contribution to 'part' of the life of every child is not performance based. The government does not employ teachers on merit. There is little regard for the unique qualities a teacher brings to the role. For the bureaucracy and the government, daily attendance suffices for teachers to be rewarded. All teachers move along the same pay scale, regardless of their contribution.

Inspectorates

From 1872 to 1983 inspectors monitored the quality of principals and teachers. The delivery of the standard instruction was a necessary part of the State school system. The measure of teacher performance and student outcomes was a matter for the inspector.

Inspectors were of the highest order, and were often distinguished graduates in arts and law. Teachers were paid a fixed salary and remuneration by way of results. Publication of their performance, prepared by inspectors, ensured an accurate classification system and guarded against improper influence in the appointment, transfer or promotion of teachers.

The role of inspector was abolished in 1983, and anti-intellectualism in various guises has since permeated The Department of Education. Enterprise agreements today place all teachers in specified categories. Ongoing debate about performance pay has been silenced by the re-introduction of permanent employment. Teacher performance cannot be measured, valuable teachers cannot be rewarded, and underperforming teachers have no incentive to improve.

The return of inspectorates and remuneration based on results are worthy of consideration. Remuneration based on student outcomes would align teacher's pedagogical practices with performance outcomes for both teacher and student.

Unions

Unions enjoy exclusive and collective bargaining rights. The natural right of principals and teachers to negotiate terms and conditions of their own employment independently is impossible to exercise within this framework of legal exclusivity. For unions, fairness means 'sameness'. Individual principals and teachers might have the right to forego union membership, but they must still abide by the collective wages and conditions negotiated by their union. Merit has no place in State schools while unions have exclusive bargaining rights. There must be an alternative to union representation for school employees.

Capabilities and Negotiated Responsibilities

Schools are responsible for the delivery of a standard curriculum. Teachers must be paid for delivering this service, provided they have the capability to do so. The salary, however, should not be the same.

An example: Two Year 4 teachers working in the same school have the same class size – 22 students – as negotiated by unions. Teacher A has 4 students with special needs, and no additional funding for support staff. Teacher B has a regular classroom. The workload of these two teachers will be different. A school in the adjoining suburb has a Year 4 teacher who has just 16 students in her class. Another school, some 200km away, has a combined Year 3-4 class of just 11 students. All four teachers will be paid the same salary because of union enterprise negotiations.

Diagram 17: Specialised Employment

Specialised Employment

Standard scales, including years of service, are reasonable. Other factors that affect teacher performance or workload must be considered in wage negotiations. Teachers with different qualifications, content specialists, teacher mentors and industry experts should have the right to negotiate terms of employment. The greater the diversity of curriculum on offer, the greater the need for employee diversity, and for individual salary negotiation.

Key Problem:

Enterprise agreements place unions in control of teacher performance.

Consequences:

- High performing teachers are not recognised for effort.
- Children are placed with teachers based on class size, not capability.
- Teachers have to work with underperforming colleagues.
- Ambitious, competent teachers are a threat to poor performers.
- Schools have a culture of secure employment not optimal service.
- Principals cannot fire underperforming teachers.
- Ambitious, high performing teachers are moved out of teaching.
- Other portfolios are affected by the complacency created by enterprise bargaining.

Key Solution:

Establish a tiered wages system. Base income on a stable curriculum, supplemented by additional services.

Principle 18:

The Flexible Home-School-Work-Life Agreement

Going with the flow is like having a PhD in purposeful immersion.

Take a drive in the city for 10 minutes in any direction and chances are you will pass a building displaying the giant gold arches. The growth of the McDonald's empire is an incredible success story. You would be correct in thinking that its success is based on a formula of hamburgers and fries. That's correct up to a point. The underlying business model, however, is the acquisition of real estate. McDonalds can be found on freeways, in major towns and cities, and in almost every country around the world.

There's one store in Richmond, with golden arches as big and bold as you would find on any outlet, but the store itself is tiny. There's barely enough seating for 10 people. There's no playground. The menu is limited in range, but as consistent as those you would find in any other McDonald's store. The same can be said for State schools. They all offer a teaching service, and they are all on valuable parcels of land, in almost every town and city in the State. Some are smaller; some offer a bigger education menu. And, although they don't have the same giant signs out the front, we can generally identify a school when we pass one.

State schools are places of government employment. For the most part, they provide a teaching service on 5 days a week, for 40 weeks of the calendar year, usually between the hours of 9.00am and 3.30pm.

There is at least one State school in every community.

There are 6.3 million people in Victoria. 3.5 million are employed full time. Of this figure, 45,500 are teachers, employed in just over 1,500 State schools. The operating hours of businesses and services that employ the 3.5 million employees are varied. Retail stores no longer operate on a 9.00am to 5.30pm schedule. Saturday morning trade has expanded to weekend trade, including all day Saturday and Sunday. Public holidays no longer apply to everyone. Fast food chains and other services, including hotlines and helplines, are open 24/7. There is never a day or a time when every business and every service is closed. Neither is there a day that every employee across the State takes off, or a time when everyone leaves work. Schools, on the other hand, are closed for 12 weeks of the year.

Our most valuable assets – State schools – are places of employment for less than 2% of Victoria's full time workers, yet the lives of Victorian families must be organised around this 2% employment model.

Students

Instruction in nominated learning areas is provided free of charge for all children attending a government school from the early years to the completion of Year 12. It is compulsory for children who are enrolled in a government school to attend during the hours of instruction. Students must plan other interests and responsibilities – including sport, part-time work, home duties and homework –around the 40-week schedule.

Homework

In the majority of schools, there is the expectation that students do homework. Although there is no legislation requiring it, schools expect parents to monitor student homework on their behalf. Time spent on homework can vary from 30 minutes per day to 4 hours or more – particularly during Years 11 and 12. The number of hours a student spends on work outside school affects other interests and responsibilities.

Family Life

Parents must manage their lives around school instructional times. Working parents with younger children might rely on before and after school care, an expense that they must cover. Childcare arrangements have to be made for 12 weeks of the year when schools are closed. These might include holiday programs, at further cost to parents, reliance on other family members, or splitting holidays between parents. Other demands from schools, including parent-teacher interviews, information evenings, committee meetings and student free days – arranged at times that suit the school – also have an impact on family life.

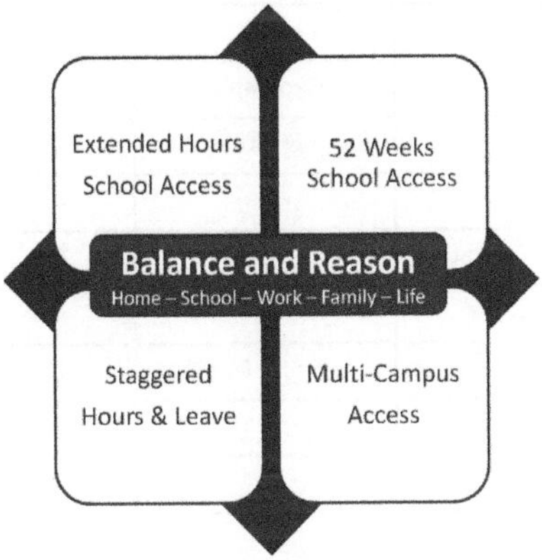

```
         Extended Hours      52 Weeks
         School Access      School Access

              Balance and Reason
           Home – School – Work – Family – Life

           Staggered         Multi-Campus
          Hours & Leave         Access
```

Diagram 18A: Scoping School Choice

Tied to the Calendar

For teachers, face-to-face classroom time is no more than 22.5 hours per week, and their attendance at school is required only when the school is open for instruction. Teachers, like most professionals, are employed for 48 weeks and are entitled to 4-weeks leave *per annum*. It is understood that teachers accrue sufficient overtime that entitles them to take 12-weeks leave instead of 4-weeks. Their leave is also dependent on the structure of the school calendar.

Flexible Schooling

Not all schools, families and communities have the same needs and lifestyles. Nevertheless, despite there being no legislation on school start and finish times, all schools remain fixed to the same industrial, monitorial system.

Learning Area	Subject	% hours per week	Hours per week
English		27%	6.5
Mathematics		18%	4.5
Science		4%	1
Humanities/Social Science	History	2%	.5
	Geography	2%	.5
	Civics & Citizenship	0	0
The Arts		4%	1
Health / Physical Education		8%	2
Languages		5%	1.25
Technology	Digital & Design	2%	.5
Time Allocated		72%	18
Time not Allocated		28%	7

Diagram 19A: Current Recommendations For Curriculum Coverage

For example, teachers' face-to-face classroom time is fixed at 22.5 hours per week. And although not all students require 13 years to achieve Year 12 standard, the year level system is more or less rigid. Families have priorities and interests that extend beyond the demands of school, but are tied to, and often encumbered by, its schedules.

Flexible work-life arrangements have been negotiated for decades, including the extension of hours for retail and other service providers. This flexibility has not been extended to schooling.

Key Problem:

The school year is inconsistent with flexible work practices.

Consequences:

- School hours contribute to peak traffic
- High out of pocket expenses for working parents who pay for out of school care.
- Holiday costs for those restricted to travelling during peak season.
- Conflict between teacher time and family time.
- Uneven distribution of workload for teachers.
- Paid work hours are not measured against performance.
- Teaching can be potentially a lifestyle, rather than a vocational choice.
- Students are bound by inflexible mandatory attendance requirements.
- 1500 valuable assets lie dormant for 12 weeks of the year.

Key Solution:

Introduce staggered timetables from 8.00am to 6.00pm – offered 52 weeks of the year.

Other possible solutions:

- Introduce summer school for extension programs and remedial teaching
- Open the schools to small businesses offering specialist services during out of school hours.
- Start and finish times should suit climate, and local industry
- Split days for teachers – all of whom are employed for either stable curriculum or other specialisms
- Students who can achieve required standard ahead of time can take time out for other interests or responsibilities – e.g. part-time work
- Design school schedules based on key stages in stable curriculum and electives, not calendar year
- Split school day into two sessions – 8.00am-2.00pm and 12.00-6.00pm

Principle 19:

Assess and Report Using More Than One Metric

Every person, every program, every philosophy, every idea, and every assessment have value – and also flaws.

Lily loved school. She completed her assignments on time, read widely and was an all-round model student – until she grew bored. In Year 7 she was reading the classics and in Year 8 she completed a certificate in photography; neither activity was a school offering. In Year 9 she was capable of completing the VCE but wasn't allowed to. By Year 10 she had a part-time job, worked as a volunteer for St. John's Ambulance and had held her own art exhibition; none of these were school offerings. She loved learning, but was constrained by the limitations of the curriculum.

Our ancestors had a vision: that every child should reach an agreed standard in reading, writing, and arithmetic, regardless of faith or socio-economic status. The significance of the vision remains. The difference between State government and non-government schooling, in terms of cost, and therefore affordability for parents, should not be a measure of any school's value. What takes place inside a school should be the true measure. Achieving an agreed standard of education gives all individuals the choice to remain within, or reach beyond, their position in life.

Broader educational options, and an extraordinary amount of

investment, have improved and expanded educational opportunities for children. Common, technical, boarding and consolidated schools, and teachers colleges were established. Pathways from primary schools to grammar schools, technical or high schools became possible. Schools evolved from the one-room structures to award winning architectural masterpieces. School attendance is now compulsory until the age of 17, and the curriculum has expanded far beyond the 3Rs. Innovations have helped many students to pursue their wider interests. There has been much to celebrate.

Our ancestors could rightly be mortified, however, that their vision has not been fully realised. The free, compulsory and secular education they envisaged has taken on a meaning all of its own. The purpose and value of their perceived standard of education was never about politics, money or faith. Quite the contrary. It was about belonging, freedom, responsibility and personal fulfilment, which an agreed standard of education in reading, writing and arithmetic would make possible. Competency in these fundamentals will always be critical for accessing broader educational options of personal choice. State schools were intended to deliver these fundamentals.

The Standard

The provision of teachers or employees to deliver the promised standard of instruction has been a constant challenge. The ideal would be a guarantee of the fundamentals for all students, so that all would then have the option of furthering their education – by way of pursuing a craft, a skill, a trade or a profession. If instruction in the fundamentals of reading, writing, and arithmetic were consistent across schools, all students could enjoy independence, responsibility, personal satisfaction and the capacity to contribute to society.

Standards of instruction in reading, writing and arithmetic have all but vanished. The Australian Curriculum, first delivered in 2009, can be adapted by States and their registered schools. These adaptations disguise the missing details within the minimum standard of instruction.

Australia's curriculum has grown in subject offerings but has shrunk in essential content. There is no nationally agreed standard of instruction in reading, writing, language conventions and numeracy. There is, however, greater choice of subjects on offer. Although choice is necessary and welcomed, the teachers responsible for the delivery of these choices are not always sufficiently experienced or qualified.

Measuring the Standard

The National Assessment Program – Literacy and Numeracy (NAPLAN) measures student capabilities in Years 3, 5, 7 and 9. The intention of NAPLAN is to measure reading, writing, language conventions (spelling, grammar, punctuation) and numeracy – the elements of standard instruction. On average, students in Year 9 have reached the age of 15. In 1872, this was the upper age at which children were entitled to participate in State school education, in order to reach the 'standard' in reading, writing and arithmetic. The difference between then and now is that in 1872, students who had already met the standard, or who could achieve the standard by other means, were not compelled to attend school. They were free to explore other educational options.

Beyond the Standard

The expansion of the curriculum and the reduction of expertise in the 3Rs have given the States almost total control of the educational choices that children to the age of 17 can access. The measure of school performance, particularly in the last decade, is evidence that centralised control of education must cease. Service providers beyond government employees from the education portfolio must be able to offer expertise and different experiences to children. Allowing families to choose a school as the provider for a stable curriculum, and to access other service providers for electives and other educational experiences would remedy this.

Employee Transitions and Pathways

In days gone by, people as young as 14, who had achieved the agreed standard of instruction, could become teachers. Compulsory education has now been extended to the age of 17. Children have until this age to reach competency in reading, writing, language conventions and numeracy. Many do not. Achievement standards have fallen, and 17-year-old students are accepted into pre-service teacher training, regardless of the standard they have reached.

The Literacy and Numeracy Test for Initial Teacher Education Students, introduced to ensure 'teachers are equipped to meet the demands of teaching', while valuable, is yet to be extended those already teaching.

After they are employed, teachers undergo performance reviews, more commonly known as peer reviews. Teachers also share the teaching of subjects such as reading, writing and numeracy. Colleagues who work together review one another. The measure of teacher performance has become totally arbitrary.

Teacher performance is the major contributing factor in student outcomes. Teachers might obtain the right to work after graduating from university, but that is not the same as obtaining the qualifications or capabilities needed to carry out the work they are employed to do.

A necessary, but absent, feature of the current State school system is a transition and pathways program, to allow teachers to transfer their skills to specialist areas, or to transfer out of teaching altogether.

Student Certificates

State control begins when a child is 6 years old. Provided children attend compulsory school education from the age of 6-17 years, they receive a Victorian Certificate of Education (VCE). It is essentially a certificate of permission to leave school, confirming 13 years of school attendance. Competent students cannot acquire a VCE ahead of time and, despite their performance, struggling students move from year to year toward the VCE.

Imagine if students could select from a range of standard certificates, and have the freedom to achieve a standard of instruction in their own time, with the flexibility to focus on other interests, such as part-time work. That would represent a genuine measure of success – for the school, the curriculum and for the student. It *is* possible.

Competence not Choice

Schools reveal their effectiveness and efficacy by properly fulfilling their mission, as expected. A three-year strategy and an annual implementation plan usually drive the school mission. All schools include the improvement of literacy and numeracy in their goals. Without an agreed standard of instruction, or an agreed schedule of regular assessment, outcomes are based purely on teacher judgement. If teachers have not achieved those standard themselves, they are certainly not equipped to measure or judge whether or not students have achieved them.

Merely teaching the standard curriculum must not be a measure of whether or not a school is suitable. Parents must be *guaranteed* the standard curriculum, regardless of the school attended. Choices must be made based on specialist options or electives a school might offer, not on its performance in teaching the fundamentals of education.

Closing the Gap

The Victorian curriculum is a slight adaptation of the Australian Curriculum. Schools and teachers can further adapt the curriculum and make decisions about resourcing, pedagogy and student support. Autonomy has value. However, autonomy over reading, writing, language conventions and numeracy literally erases any and all ability to measure accurately, compare, deliver or fund instruction in schools.

When a national curriculum can be changed at the local level, it is no longer a national curriculum. It has no value. Any attempt to 'close the gap' must come only after determining the details of the gap. This is not possible without an agreed standard of achievement.

The Unknown

Schools often showcase Year 12 results and the students who are accepted into universities. Some things are never attributed to schools: the number of students who later drop out of tertiary and further education, particularly during their first year; employment pathways;

unemployment figures; welfare dependency; or crime. Comparing these figures across schools and school systems, including non-government and home-based schooling would be of further value. Without these vital statistics there is no way of identifying real return on investment.

Beyond Measure

Education is the wealth of knowledge acquired after studying subject matter, and by experiencing life lessons, through instruction or composed literature – all of which provides an understanding of something.

We are all educated. We are certainly not, however – and could never be – educated in the same way. We all have different methods of receiving, processing, producing, sharing and using what we know, understand and do.

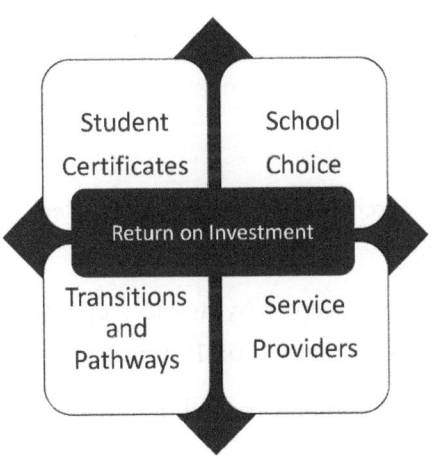

Diagram 19B: Service Provision Measure

The establishment of free, compulsory and secular education made a great deal of sense. If we returned to an agreed stable curriculum, a measure of genuine success would be possible: in teacher performance, student performance, funding to close any measured gaps, and opportunities for those who excel. Students and teachers should also have available transitions and pathways to go beyond that: to access experts in fields of interest; to take advantage of extra-curricular opportunities; to choose from a range of certificates, not limited to year levels; and to have options other than compulsory schooling, if course work has been completed.

Compulsory schooling has only one metric: the theft of freedom. There is no other situation in life – with the exception of incarceration – that compels physical presence in the same way that compulsory schooling does.

Key Problem:

Year 12 is the yardstick for workplace value and further study.

Consequences:

- Students receive a certificate of leaving regardless of capability.
- Universities accept 17-year old students whose standard is less than a 14-year-old of 150 years ago.
- Increasing compulsory school age reduces or disguises unemployment figures.
- A national curriculum to Year 10 limits choice and States retain control over content.

- Soft skills have no value and cannot be measured.
- Teachers are paid a salary for attendance not performance.

Key Solution:

Certificates of achievement for stable curriculum, curriculum specialisms and community electives - not year level.

Principle 20:

Fund Suitability: Collect the Interest

You can't choreograph the future; you can, however, be prepared for it.

Jessica has four sons. Three of them attended the local State primary school. Her youngest had behaviour problems at school. Assessments were done and Jessica was told he had ADHD. Interventions failed; his behaviour worsened. He was moved three times before he eventually settled down in a school, where he stayed until Year 11. In Years 7 to 12, the other three boys attended six different schools between them. Two were State secondary colleges, and four were non-government schools. The differences between the boys, their interests, and their academic rigour presented the underlying challenges in finding a school that would suit them. One son was recognised as gifted during his early years at school; one wanted to be a tradesman; the other had an interest in film and television. Outside school, their lives were also busy – with involvement in a band, an online business, part-time jobs, and membership of an activist group, among others.

On 1 January 2019, the implementation of the National School Reform Agreement (NSRA) came into force. It has one objective: 'Australian schooling provides a high quality and equitable education for all students'.

Achievement of the NSRA faces three major challenges. First, the agreement contains no definition of education. Second, most of the national policy initiatives required to achieve its single objective are subject to approval by the Education Council. Third, without approval of these national initiatives, there is room for ongoing disagreement over this country's philosophy – its beliefs, values and understandings with respect to education and, in particular, school education.

In other words, the NSRA is a living document, but one that has not yet articulated clearly what Australian schooling actually provides. In a context where there is no definition of education and no philosophical agreement, it could be suggested that we are in a dire position.

This document, however, affords a rare opportunity. Rather than seeing these issues as problematic, and instead taking an optimistic vantage point, there is an opening for total system wide reform for school education. Redistribution of funding is key to such an opportunity.

Paying for Schools

The main sources of funding to schools are the state and federal governments. Although constitutional control of schools and schooling rests with the State, the federal government has become increasingly involved in schooling, largely due to the redistribution of taxes collected at the federal level.

Other sources of funding to schools are grants, donations, fundraising efforts, voluntary contributions and fees. Although the State school system offers free instruction, there are costs associated with learning, and all schools expect or require some form of financial contribution from families.

Federal Funding

A School Resource Standard (SRS) is an estimate of public funding required to meet the educational needs of students. The most recent review of education, Gonski 2.0, has made recommendations on the SRS and additional loadings required for students and schools considered to be disadvantaged.

A base amount is established for every student. For primary students it is just over $11,000; for each secondary school student, just over $14,000. This base amount is adapted according to each school community's capacity to contribute to the operational costs of the school.

The Socio Economic Status (SES) of the school, currently determined by each student's residential address, is used to calculate the capacity to pay. The higher the SES, the greater the amount subtracted from the base amount. Government schools and specialised non-government schools are not affected by this reduction.

By 2023, calculations will reflect two distinct funding responsibilities. In line with the Australian Constitution, government schools will be predominantly funded by the States and Territories (80%) and non-government schools will be predominantly funded by the Commonwealth (80%).

Additional Loadings

Additional loadings for students are paid for the following reasons:

Disability: Approval is determined by the Nationally Consistent Collection of Data for Students with a Disability (NCCD).

Low English Language Proficiency: Students coming from backgrounds other than English-speaking and having at least one parent who completed school education only to Year 9 or below.

Aboriginal and Torres Strait Islanders: The amount of extra funding for each student depends on the proportion of Indigenous students in the school.

Socio Economic Disadvantage: This is a measure of the occupational and educational status of students' parents.

School Location Loading: For schools in regional and remote areas.

School Size Loading: For medium, small and very small schools. Eligible schools are those with a population of up to 300 students for primary, and 700 students in secondary.

Distribution

The Commonwealth has no constitutional control over schools and schooling; neither does it have constitutional control over compulsory school age. It does, however, have constitutional control over the distribution of taxes it collects. Currently all Commonwealth funding for school education goes directly to each State or Territory, who then distribute funding to each school.

Compulsory Attendance

A parent with a child aged 0-5 years can choose whether or not to use childcare. The Federal government makes financial contributions to assist families in the cost of care, regardless of the registered service they choose. When children turn 17, they can choose to earn a full time living or enrol in higher education. If higher education is their choice, the federal government will provide financial support, regardless of the career chosen.

It is compulsory for every child between the ages of 6 and 17 years to attend school. If a State government school is selected, that same government will provide the facilities and the staff. Where the parent chooses a non-government school, there is no provision of facilities or staff.

State Funding

At the State level, schools receive funding based on what is called the Student Resource Package. It is calculated by the demographic of students – in other words, the family profile, the number of students enrolled, the school's location and the level of disability among students. Constitutionally the State is responsible for the provision of buildings, grounds, and employees for the delivery of the standard curriculum. Student-teacher ratios, negotiated by the union, have a major effect of the cost of operating schools.

Reward for Disadvantage

Additional funding is limited to agreed loading types, determined predominantly by parent profile. Unless they present with a disability, children's needs or capabilities are irrelevant. It is implied, for example, that low income or vocational choice means a low IQ. Similarly, being born to parents of non-English speaking background implies a disability. The student's capability is not factored into the funding model. And, clearly, there is no inherent value placed on a student being responsible, gifted or talented.

Of further concern, additional funding does not result in the provision of expert teachers to cater for a school's student loading profile.

Parent and Child

Parents currently may choose between government and non-government schools for their child. Factors affecting this choice might be income and place of residence. They also have the option of home schooling. Most non-government schools are established on religious values and beliefs. In other words, the exercise of religious freedom gives parents wider choice in the context of schooling.

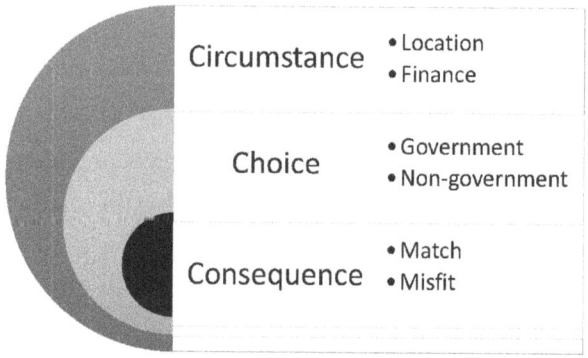

Diagram 20A: Limited School Choice

For families with children who have a disability, or diverse ability – including those who are gifted or have a genuine passion in an area of potential expertise – their choice remains limited to government or non-government schooling.

The right for all children to enrol in a mainstream school is important for reasons of inclusion and acceptance. In many ways, however, it has fallen short of giving disabled, as well as gifted and highly focussed children, the education that is most suitable for their specific needs or desires.

At the State level, parents and children are guaranteed a place to attend and to receive instruction or teaching. The school determines the distribution of funds, decides on its teaching staff, and determines the curriculum. There is a complete disconnect between the family profile, which determines funding, and the services provided.

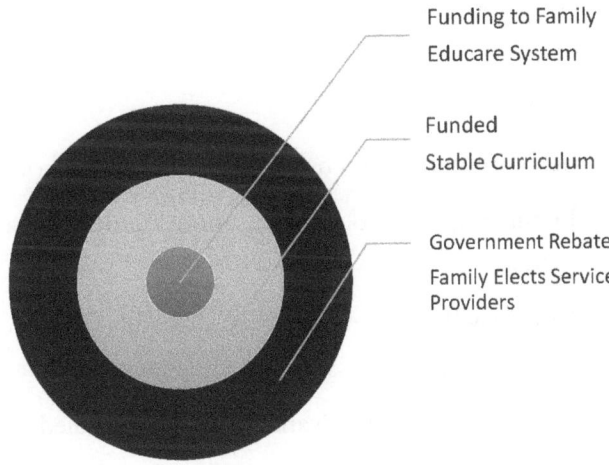

Diagram 20B: National 'Educare' Option

Funding the family instead of funding the school could provide a direct link between the service provider and the recipient of the service – that is, the family. Perhaps Australia should consider an 'Educare' system – similar to Medicare. Commonwealth funding would then be available for all children who receive an agreed stable curriculum – at key stages rather than during the years of compulsory attendance – in literacy, numeracy, health and physical education, and studies in Western civilisation. Additional funding, with rebates, could then be linked to income for electives and specialised teachers. Education funding would no longer be limited to an education portfolio, but would be distributed more broadly across a range of service providers and multiple portfolios.

Key Problem:

Funding is distributed to schools not to students.

Consequences:

- School funding does not guarantee a standard of education.
- Funding operates on a deficit model rather than an incentive model.
- Parents with children who have gifts and talents are financially disadvantaged.
- It is implied that disadvantage can be remedied with funding.
- Teacher quality is not linked to funding.
- There is no reward or consequence linked to school or teacher performance.
- Underperforming schools receive bonuses.
- Formulas are not personalised.
- School choice has major limitations.

Key Solution:

Introduce national 'Educare' funding, to provide rebates for families to access registered service providers across multiple portfolios.

Other Possible Solutions:

- Provide registered service providers – e.g. fitness instructors – with access to schools, to deliver services

- Redistribute grants received by not-for-profit organisations to service organisations, including Scouts and St Johns Ambulance.

- Introduce a 'gap year' in Years 9 and 10 (Stage 5) to enable students to pursue other interests prior to Years 11 and 12.

A Final Note

The foundations of the future were laid down centuries ago. Just as past philosophers, almoners, malenders and explorers still influence our lives today, our presence will have historical significance for those to come. Everyone has some influence on others. The process of learning and teaching is the genesis of all the difference a life can make.

I have a vision for a different future in learning and teaching. It involves repurposing the school system and legislating reforms that have never been attempted before. It will attract both praise and cynicism. Critics will point out its flaws; proponents will support it and contribute their own vision. This is exciting.

If all the answers lay in the palm of one hand, there would be no reason to speak; the all-knowing cannot hear.

I am optimistic that optimism itself – the doctrine of hope – will find its way inside the heart and mind of every individual who has a genuine regard for learning and teaching. For any aspect of this vision to have life and breath, there must be noise, laughter, humour, and robust interaction.

Now that you have read some, or all, of this book, know that your influence has power. Be disruptive, and be confident in your disruption of current thought and practice. Share your agreement with, or your rejection of, what you have read. The greater the noise, the more willingly other voices will join in.

Abnegation of responsibility deserves no oxygen.

Acknowledgements

The Rotary Club of Melbourne was chartered on 21 April 1921 as the first Rotary Club in Australia. It was founded on the principles of integrity, opportunity, service and success, and it is an honour and privilege to be worthy of membership. Just as importantly, I am an enthusiastic student of some of the most extraordinary gentlemen in Victoria, with whom I share Rotary membership. My sincere gratitude goes, in particular, to Hon. Gerald Ashman, Clive Weeks AO, David Beanland AO, Rev. Colin Honey and Bruce Davidson.

Research is at its best when it is shared and challenged. Excello on Spring Street, is a hive of activity, intellect, friendship and mentoring. I am sincerely grateful, especially, to Dennis Troedel KSJ, Stewart McArthur AM, Cameron Clarke and Peter Kelly.

Patriotism should never be taken lightly. To Charryce Nixon-Luke and Sam Muscat, thank you.

We are so very fortunate to learn from dedicated researchers, authors and historians. Without their work, this book would have no value. My sincere gratitude goes to Geoffrey Blainey AC and Anna Blainey for your generosity and friendship.

To Anthony, for trusting I could write something, and to Janette Parr, my editor and friend, you work magic with your craft to ensure the clarity my readers deserve.

To my extraordinary daughters Somraudee and Sze Ting. You weren't born under my heart, but in it. Thank you for making me a mum.

To Mum, Dad and Craig, our resilience binds us.

To Clifton. I love you

To Kaye, Mary, Margie and Sandra. Thank you for your patience and for standing beside the most inspirational men on this journey – Peter McCall OAM, Alistair Urquhart, Howard Hutchins and Ian McIntyre.

God Bless.